THE MAKING OF
MUSICAL
INSTRUMENTS

BY

THOMAS CAMPBELL YOUNG

Essay Index Reprint Series

BOOKS FOR LIBRARIES PRESS

FREEPORT, NEW YORK

First Published 1939
Reprinted 1969

INTERNATIONAL STANDARD BOOK NUMBER:
0-8369-1317-5

LIBRARY OF CONGRESS CATALOG CARD NUMBER:
79-90698

PRINTED IN THE UNITED STATES OF AMERICA
BY
NEW WORLD BOOK MANUFACTURING CO., INC.
HALLANDALE, FLORIDA 33009

INTRODUCTION

MUSIC in its widest sense embraces several distinct participants. The composer sets down on paper a symphony, a song, or a dance tune. The publisher prints and distributes the composition. The performer, if an instrumentalist, plays it on 'an instrument of musick', and an audience listens, and, incidentally, 'pays the bill'.

During the last few years thousands of boys and girls have both heard and seen orchestral instruments played: thousands more have at least heard them broadcast. It is not to be doubted that most of these listeners must have asked at one time or another, 'How do they work? and how are they made?'

'Why does the trombone player keep on moving his slide, while the trumpeter doesn't *seem* to move his instrument at all?'

'How is it that an organist with only three "sets of piano keys" can produce hundreds of different effects?'

'And however does the wind manage to get to the right pipes?'

There will always be more questions than answers in the world, but I hope, and, indeed, *promise* to answer, during the course of this work, a great number of questions which youthful listeners have asked.

It is my purpose to study the manufacture and the construction of musical instruments: to find out how they are made, and how they work. There is such a variety of instruments, however, that it will not be possible to consider them all, but we shall visit many factories where we hope to see the manufacture of *pianofortes, violins, wood-wind and brass instruments,* and, finally, *the organ.*

In modern industry the machine has replaced almost entirely the handcraftsman, but it will be found that in the making of musical instruments much of the traditional

Introduction

handicraft still survives, and it is to this survival, rather than to the encroachment of mechanical inventions, that our attention will be directed.

This book should find its way into the class-rooms of those schools where senior pupils are working 'along practical lines'. It can be used as a technical reader, for the information is authoritative, i.e. *it presents only facts*; the information has been taken 'at first hand' from the expert at his work.

The one proviso is that practice and precedent are bound to vary somewhat between manufacturers of a similar type of instrument. But in the main these variations are negligible.

Since we are dealing with actual practice in modern factories, it seems reasonable to assume, first, that the book will be welcomed, as a change, by teachers and scholars alike, who have grown weary of the existing type of reader, still so common in many schools; and second, that the inside glimpses here afforded, of craftsmen plying their trade, will help to enlighten, to interest, and so to prepare the adolescent for the world and the work awaiting him when school-days are over.

To conclude, it is my hope that, considered solely from the standpoint of music, a study of the manufacture and behaviour of some of our finest musical instruments will lead to a growing interest in the part they play as units in the great realm of Music which, I venture to assert, is the noblest of the arts.

To the performer, such knowledge is of paramount importance, to the listener it cannot fail to give an added stimulus.

ACKNOWLEDGEMENTS

(TO ORIGINAL EDITION)

I WISH to record my real indebtedness and sincere thanks to all the manufacturers whose factories I visited, for so kindly allowing me to occupy the time of their managers, foremen, and craftsmen, experts all, who spent for my sole benefit countless hours and much personal effort.

The innumerable facts and processes hereafter described were all taken directly from the makers themselves, and the reader will not have proceeded far in this book before beginning to appreciate how deeply I am indebted to all those who have so carefully, and often so patiently, helped me to understand the processes they were completing.

Another outstanding fact which one cannot help but notice is the extreme care and thoroughness expended on every instrument at each stage of its evolution. This will enable us to understand why, *to-day, musical instruments of British manufacture are unsurpassed by those of any other makers in the world.*

In particular, I wish to thank personally, and sincerely, the following, each of whom it was my great pleasure and privilege to know. (They are placed in the order in which I met them.)

Mr. Hubert J. Foss, who first mooted the idea that I should undertake this work, which, may I say, appalled me by its magnitude.

Mr. Ernest White, of the Music Industries Council, who introduced me to most of the manufacturers I met.

Mr. W. S. Strohmenger, of John Strohmenger & Sons (pianoforte manufacturers). It was through the courtesy of Mr. Strohmenger that I spent many pleasant hours in his factory.

Mr. A. E. Healey, of Herburger Brooks Pianoforte Actions, Keyboards, &c. (by whose courtesy I reproduce the pianoforte action shown on page 35). Mr. Healey conducted me, personally, over his entire factory and described in detail each and every process I have recorded in his particular department.

Acknowledgements

Messrs. H. S. Clark, J. H. Clark, and C. Clark, and also *Mr. H. H. Sanders*—foundry foreman—of Messrs. J. Clark & Sons (makers of pianoforte frames), by whose courtesy the photograph reproduced for the frontispiece was taken, and from whom I obtained particulars of the various processes of pianoforte frame manufacture.

Mr. Herbert J. Brinsmead, who kindly allowed me to see and describe the making of wrapped strings, and who also showed me the many kinds of felt and baize which are used in the manufacture of pianofortes.

Mr. W. Rushworth and his entire staff, and also *Mr. Bird,* of Messrs. Rushworth & Dreaper (organ builders, &c.), Liverpool.

Only those who have stayed 'under the wing' of Mr. Rushworth can realize the 'all-in' quality of his hospitality.

To Mr. Bird I am indebted for the full story of violin manufacture.

Mr. Chas. E. Timms and all his foremen and experts, of Messrs. Besson, Ltd. (makers of musical instruments), by whose courtesy the reproductions of the brass instruments are copied.

Mr. Timms was most helpful to me in every way. It was by his permission that I saw and described the manufacture of reeds, in addition to that of brass instruments.

Mr. Ralph Hawkes, Mr. A. Blaikley, and all their technical experts, especially the wood-wind and brass tuners of Messrs. Boosey & Hawkes (notably Mr. Manton-Myatt), by whose courtesy I was allowed to describe the manufacture of wood-wind instruments and also the deep-drawing method described on pages 88–95.

By the courtesy of Mr. Ralph Hawkes, too, the Hammond Organ was demonstrated and explained to me.

Mr.. Herbert Norman and all the assistants under him—particularly *Mr. E. D. Sayer*—of Messrs. Hill, Norman & Beard (organ manufacturers). It was by the courtesy and great

Acknowledgements

kindness of Mr. Norman that I was enabled to spend hour upon hour—whole days, in fact—encroaching upon the valuable time of a very busy firm.

Mr. Sayer, technical expert, helped me perhaps more than any other individual I met. He thought I was 'a brave man', to use *his* words—'even to hope to attempt the colossal task of describing a modern electric organ'; and I do not hesitate to admit that but for his invaluable help over many a hurdle I might never have completed the course.

Lastly, I wish to thank, and to commend for his 'workmanship', *Mr. Alan Curwell*, who prepared my drawings and sketches for reproduction; the merit of his work 'speaks' for itself.

T. C. Y.

January 1938.

CONTENTS

Contents

Contents

LIST OF ILLUSTRATIONS

List of Illustrations

List of Illustrations

List of Illustrations

THE PIANOFORTE

THE pianoforte, more commonly called the piano, derives its name from two Italian words, *piano*, meaning 'soft', and *forte*, meaning 'loud'. It was so named because its tone could be either diminished or increased. Its true forerunner was the clavichord, which, like the piano, is a descendant of the dulcimer. The notes on the clavichord

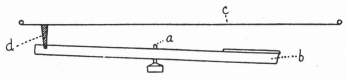

FIG. 1. *Key and tangent.*
a, *Balance pin*; b, *Key*; c, *String*; d, *Tangent.*

were produced by small tangents or slender blades of brass (Fig. 1). The tangent, on striking the string, which was usually a fine brass wire, did not rebound, but remained in contact with it, as shown, 'stopping' the string and causing it to vibrate in two segments, one of which was damped, or muffled, by a piece of cloth.

Its tone was decidedly limited in power but within that limit very fine gradations of touch, and consequently of tone, were possible. The tangents made a clicking noise on impact, which might have been disturbing to a critical ear.

But the point we wish to stress is that *it could not play loudly.* In brief, it had no *forte.*

The harpsichord, which immediately preceded the pianoforte, worked on a totally different principle. Its tone was produced by a 'jack', which was really a mechanical plectrum whereby the string was actually plucked by a projecting piece of quill: leather, or brass, was sometimes substituted. Though many ingenious devices were tried in an endeavour to modify the tone, none of them can be said to have been successful.

The harpsichord *could not produce a soft tone*. In short—it had no *piano*.

Most people have both seen and heard a modern pianoforte. There are, of course, many distinct types of piano, of which the full concert-grand takes precedence, and whose length is eight and a half feet. There are many varieties of smaller grands, of lengths ranging from six and a half to four feet. All these have horizontal or flat bodies supported on legs, and their strings, frame, and soundboard lie parallel with the floor.

The upright, or vertical piano, however, is probably the most familiar. We will consider, therefore, the construction of this model, and so we may form a good idea of the way in which other types of piano are made.

Let us now go to the piano itself for a brief preliminary survey. That part which we actually see is the *case* which encloses and protects the instrument. It is beautifully designed and finished, and presents a pleasing appearance, but is little concerned with the production of sound. If the piano is open, the keys, usually black and white, can be seen. Actually, they are only the visible portion of the *keyboard* proper, the remainder being hidden by the front part of the case.

The notes are sounded by striking or depressing the keys. These communicate the 'blow' to the hammers, and they in turn strike the strings, which are thus made to vibrate and produce the sound. Now open the top to see, and hear, what happens when a key is depressed—and held down by the finger. The hammer moves forward, strikes the wires or *strings*, and immediately rebounds. At the moment of striking, the damper, a small felt pad which normally presses on the strings, is released. The note is heard clearly for a while, but gradually diminishes as the strings come to rest.

Strike another note, but this time release the key almost immediately and observe how the damper automatically returns to its normal position, 'stopping' the strings, and terminating, not quite, but almost immediately, their vibrations and, consequently, the note itself. This mechanical part of the instrument within the case is known as the *action*, and any tuner would remove it quite easily if you were to ask him.

Similarly, the front of the case can be taken out; simply turn the two catches at either end, move the panel slightly outwards, and then lift it clear of the remainder. You will now be able to see part of the curved metal framework. This is made of iron and is of great strength. It is called simply the *frame*, and it plays an important part in the construction of the instrument. Behind the strings you may be able to distinguish a varnished wooden board. Actually, this is one side of the *sound-board*, which determines very largely the tone-quality of the instrument.

Now notice, more particularly, the wires or *strings* as they are called, and how, at the right-hand end, they are very short and fine. These give the high or treble notes and are grouped in threes, each individual hammer striking a group of three simultaneously. Proceeding towards the left, you should notice that from a certain point the strings are grouped in pairs, whilst steadily increasing, from left to right, in length and thickness. Approaching the extreme left end of the piano, the strings, still increasing, are now single: i.e. only one string is provided for each note. If you play one of these, you will find it rich and deep. These are the bass (pronounced 'base') strings. They are heavily wrapped—more so than the duple strings—but we shall learn the reason for this later (p. 24) The hammers here, too, are much larger than those at the treble end. Notice how cleverly the iron pegs are arranged; these are turned by the tuner when he comes to restore the notes to their true pitch.

If the instrument is not of modern design, the wires may be strung perpendicularly and parallel to one another, but in a modern instrument they will be so arranged that the wires in

3

one group cross, without actually touching, those of another; the piano is then said to be 'overstrung'.

While the top is open, press down the right pedal, and all the dampers will be automatically released from the strings, which are then free to vibrate when struck by the hammers. This pedal is usually called the *loud pedal*, but a better name would be the *sustaining* pedal. The left, or *soft pedal*, might next be depressed to see what effect it has upon the mechanism and the tone. In a modern instrument, the entire set of hammers will be moved inwards, automatically, so that these lie closer to the strings, thus shortening the length, and thereby decreasing the force of the hammer blows. The frame and the sound-board are securely fastened to the *back* of the instrument, but we cannot see the back itself.

The main constituents of the piano, then, are the case, frame, sound-board, keyboard, action, and strings.

We are now going to visit one or two large factories to follow the evolution of the pianoforte through all the stages of its construction, from raw material to finished article. It would be very difficult to determine just where the construction of a piano begins, for, as we have seen, it consists of many components.

On arriving at the factory we are conducted to a department where the sound-boards are made. Here are the 'boards' just as they are received by the maker. They are already prepared, being made of Rumanian pine which has been seasoned. Each board consists of a number of narrow strips which, after being 'shot'—i.e. having their edges perfectly trued up—are glued edge to edge and planed on both sides. The board is therefore composite and is quite thin, though not of even thickness, for at one end it measures three-eighths of an inch while at the other it is five-sixteenths, tapering gradually in thickness.

In the piano the thicker wood will help to resonate the high or treble notes, while the thinner end will lie adjacent to the bass strings. The strips or pieces which comprise it have been selected with great care. The grain is perfectly straight and there are no knots or blemishes whatever. Each individual piece has been carefully selected and matched, and has a similar annual growth. In short, everything has been done which might preserve the homogeneity of the composite board.

The maker now selects one of these composite boards and places it for a certain period in a heating chamber. He has a very particular reason for doing so. He wants to drive out every particle of moisture from the wood, for on the success of this the value of the next process will depend.

While still unnaturally dry, and before it can re-absorb any moisture from the atmosphere, the board is placed on a kind of bench, which is slightly hollowed, and a number of ribs made of spruce or pine are glued across the grain of the board parallel to one another. These ribs are kept in place in a very curious way. Curved sticks, rather like bows without strings, and called 'go-bars', are inserted between the 'ceiling' and the table (see Fig. 2, p. 6, which shows a number of these 'go-bars' in use). In the case of the ribs, many more would be inserted, for each rib would have twelve to fifteen of them.

When the glue is set, the *sound-board*, as it is now called, is left to season for a considerable time. As it re-absorbs from the atmosphere its natural quota of moisture, the original board begins to warp, and, in doing so, exerts a considerable tension on the restraining ribs. Thus there occurs what might be termed a static tension, or continuous strain. It is this condition of conflicting forces which gives to the board its sounding properties, or, to use a technical phrase, its *sympathetic resonance*.

If the sound-board is carefully made of selected and seasoned wood, it should last a life-time. If, on the other hand, the work is done cheaply or hurriedly, its life may be over within three or four years.

The ribs are now tapered towards both ends (Fig. 3, p. 7). In

5

the diagram the board has been stood on edge to show the arrangement of the ribs. Note the perfectly straight grain and also the curvature of the board and of the ribs themselves. The wooden buttons are reinforcements which are screwed

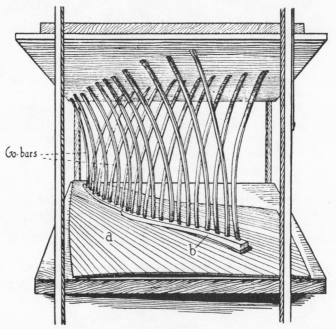

FIG. 2. *Bridge being glued to Sound-board.*
a, *Sound-board*; b, *Bridge*.

through the board to the bridges, which we shall see in a moment.

The next process is the mounting of the *bridges*, which are glued to the plain side of the sound-board. (Fig. 2, above, shows the method of mounting the curved sticks holding down the bridge while the glue is setting. Fig. 4, p. 7, shows the

6

board lying horizontally.) Note the ends of the ribs on the under side. Besides being curved, the thickness of the larger or main bridge is varied in such a way that, although its outer

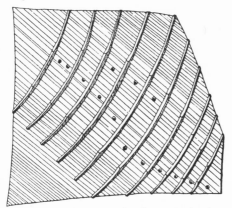

Fig. 3. *Sound-board, showing the ribs, mounted and tapered.*

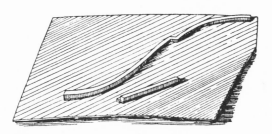

Fig. 4. *Sound-board, showing the bridges. The smaller is the 'floating bridge'.*

surface is flat, its inner side is curved to fit exactly the arc-shape or convex curve of the sound-board. This can be seen quite clearly in the diagram (Fig. 4).

Since the bridge is raised, and the taut strings will later pass

7

over it, it will transmit their vibrations to the sound-board, which by its sympathetic resonance will 'magnify' the sound and add greatly to its audible duration. In the overstrung models, a second or bass bridge is necessary to take the heavier and longer strings, and in order that this should not be too near the edge of the sound-board, where the resonance is more restricted, a device termed a 'floating' bridge is mounted near the lower extremity of the sound-board (Fig. 5). After

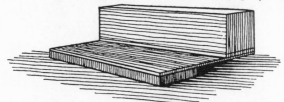

FIG. 5. *Floating bridge (not yet prepared to receive the bridge-pins and strings).*

being 'cleaned up' and varnished, the finished sound-board is now fitted to the *back*, which is a very strongly constructed wooden frame.

The ribbed side is placed inwards and the whole securely fastened, being both glued and screwed to the back. To use the maker's own words, where he is concerned with the resonance of his instrument, he 'prefers gluing to screwing'. One curious thing he mentions is the fact that sound travels along the grain six times more quickly than across it.

And now we may have to pay a visit to another factory, where 'frames' are made. The *frame* (Fig. 6, p. 9) is that part of the piano on which the strings are stretched. It is often cast from the maker's own pattern by a firm which specializes in this particular work. Some manufacturers, however, leave the pattern to the frame-maker, who designs a frame of his own.

Metal-founding involves two separate processes, namely,

moulding, when the shape of a pattern is impressed in a mould of damp sand, and *casting*, whereby the pattern is removed from the mould, which is then filled with molten metal,

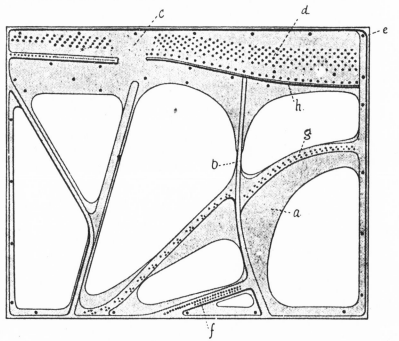

FIG. 6. *Frame for an upright overstrung piano.*

a, *Web*; b, *Bar*; c, *Plank*; d, *Wrest-pin bush holes*; e, *Countersunk screw-holes for screwing down the frame*; f, *Bass pins on pinning table*; g, *Treble section.*

poured into it through a prepared channel. The liquid metal assumes the shape defined by the mould, and, on cooling and solidifying, retains that shape when removed from the mould.

The original pattern is made of wood and from this a duplicate in metal is cast. This becomes the pattern from

9

which all subsequent frames are cast. Since metal contracts on cooling, a 'shrinkage' allowance must be made when preparing the pattern. The original one of wood must be slightly larger than the iron pattern, which in turn must be larger than the casting to be made from it. The draughtsman, therefore, in making his drawings, must provide for a double allowance, for contraction: first, for the casting of the metal pattern, and second, for the final casting of the frame. Thus, he prepares a design of the actual size the frame is to be. This is known as the frame-drawing, and from it he makes a contraction-drawing in which all measures are altered proportionately to allow for the shrinkage. (The actual amount is $\frac{1}{8}$ in. per foot for each contraction, i.e. $\frac{1}{4}$ in. altogether.)

The pattern-maker receives this drawing and proceeds to carry out its stipulations. First, he starts his 'foundation' or 'plate', using pine or mahogany, well-seasoned, of straight grain, and free from knots. All joints are strongly made, being either tongued and grooved or 'half lapped'. The whole structure is designed for strength and for resistance to warping or weakening of any kind. This foundation work is 'cleaned' and gauged to the required thickness, and on it the pattern-maker proceeds to build up those parts which stand out in greater relief (see Fig. 6, p. 9), such as the bridges, pinning-tables, and bars. This work, although carried out in pine, demands, to use the craftsman's own words, 'all the time absolute accuracy'. The parts to be added are glued and in some cases screwed also. When the pattern is finally completed and 'finished', it is a fine example of the pattern-maker's art. Before it leaves the 'shop' it is painted or treated with a special preparation to protect the wood from the action of the moisture in the damp sand.

The mould is usually fashioned in special sand or loam, moistened to give it a certain amount of cohesion. It is contained in a 'box', generally of iron (see Fig. 7, p. 11) and consisting of two halves, upper and lower. These fit exactly together, but can be taken apart to give access to the mould, which is itself made in two separate parts.

A pattern of the article to be made is placed in the sand in the lower half—called the 'drag'—and then the top or 'cope' is closed down and further sand placed in the upper half of the

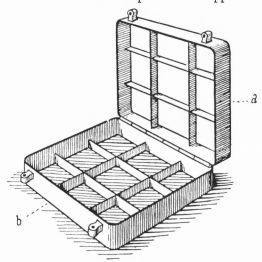

FIG. 7. *Moulding Box.*
a, *Rake (or top)*; b, *Drag.*

box, until the pattern is totally immersed and the sand level with the top rim of the box.

When the moist sand has been tightly packed all round the pattern and has literally taken its impression, the cope is lifted, the pattern is removed, and the two halves of the mould carefully 'touched up' where necessary. The cope is replaced and 'clamped down' and the molten metal is poured into the shape left in the sand by the pattern. This is called 'casting'. The metal enters by a mouth-piece or tunnel, which is funnel-shaped to facilitate pouring and to avoid waste.

The molten metal completely fills the mould and so assumes its shape. On cooling, it sets hard, or solidifies. The cope is raised once more and the casting removed for 'cleaning up' and finishing.

Moulding.

We are now conducted to the foundry, which is a very large building, measuring somewhere about two hundred and eighty feet by thirty. The whole of the floor is covered to a considerable depth with black sand. The moulders are preparing the moulds into which, later, they will pour the molten metal. The ordinary 'floor-sand', as it is termed, consists of sand or loam which has been continuously used for casting.

The factory is subdivided into bays each of which will accommodate some eight or nine moulds. The boxes which are to contain the moulds are hinged together and fitted so that they can be strongly clamped when closed.

The drag lies on the deep sand which is 'damped down' every morning to keep it moist. A gallon of water—approximately—is sprinkled to every hundredweight of floor-sand, the amount of water used varying slightly according to atmospheric conditions.

The moulder first proceeds to prepare his 'bed'. He sieves a quantity of coarse sand through a half-inch mesh. He takes up another sieve having a three-eighth-of-an-inch mesh and sprinkles another layer of floor-sand over the first. A third, ten-hole, sieve is then used (i.e. the apertures are one-tenth of an inch square). He now 'strikes his bed off', to quote his own words, using a 'strickle' or flat piece of wood to scrape off the surplus sand.

He then takes a twelve-hole sieve, but this time he uses a very special preparation known as 'facing' sand, which is composed of a mixture of floor-sand, new loam, and a small proportion of finely powdered coal-dust. This facing sand has a special purpose to fulfil. It protects the mould from the natural tendency of the molten metal to 'search' into the sand. The foreman goes into technical details, which are a little beyond the scope of our present study, but, put simply, its real purpose is to protect the mould surface from the fury of the molten metal by withstanding and absorbing the shock and the intense heat. The chief ingredient concerned is the carbon in the coal-dust. The moulder finally shakes a fine sprinkling of parting-sand through a sifting bag and the bed is ready to receive the pattern.

The pattern itself is of iron cast from the original wood pattern, but very carefully hand-finished and filed, for a pattern must be 'clean' to produce a good result.

The next process is that of 'bedding-in'. The moulder takes the pattern frame, which previously has been coated with a special preparation, probably of the shellac type—to prevent the sand from sticking to it—and places it face downwards on the prepared bed, taking extreme care to see that he has sufficient room for running in the metal when the casting is done. He then proceeds to knock the frame into the sand, using a large wooden mallet and tapping the pattern now in one place, now another, to ensure that it sinks evenly into the soft sand. When the pattern has sunk sufficiently, he goes down on hands and knees and packs the sand carefully round and over the frame, and then with an iron rammer he rams the sand all round the pattern as a preliminary to 'making his joint'. He then steps on to the mould and begins a process known as 'treading in'. It really ought to be termed 'jumping in' or 'hopping in', for the moulder, placing his two feet together— 'toes in'—proceeds to hop, like a sparrow, a step at a time, making a row of footmarks from end to end of the moulding. He begins another row and completes row after row until he has traversed the whole surface of the mould. He then starts in a direction at right-angles to the last to 'jump a row', and another, until he again covers the entire surface with foot-prints.

He now takes off the superfluous sand with a shovel and by

means of a moulder's trowel proceeds to sweep his joint', making sure that the sand round the pattern is in 'sound condition'.

He tests the whole 'bedding' of the pattern by tapping it all over: he can tell by the sound whether there is absolute contact between the pattern and the sand at every point.

When finally satisfied that all parts of the pattern are truly embedded, he sprinkles on a very thin layer of fine 'parting sand'. This is used to prevent the two halves of the mould from adhering. He has, of course, covered both the pattern and the sand in between with parting-sand. He now takes a pair of bellows and blows off the sand which covers the surface of the pattern, leaving it clean again, but the parting-sand adheres to the surrounding sand—which is moist—of the mould. He then sprinkles the very slightest layer of parting-sand over the pattern itself.

He now begins a process which is similar to that of 'preparing the bed', but this time the various processes are in the reverse order. He sieves a layer of facing-sand and afterwards cleans the edges of the 'drag' ready for the cope, which is closed down.

He inserts three, four, or five 'runner sticks', which are cylindrical bars of iron and each of which when later withdrawn will leave a channel or tunnel from the upper surface to the various parts of the mould, through which the metal can be poured when the casting is done. He now proceeds to fill in the cope, being very careful to 'tuck under the stays' so as to ensure that there will be no swelling of the casting through weakly rammed spots.

He rams down the sand, until the box is completely filled, with a considerable amount of sand to spare. He removes with a shovel all superfluous sand. The runner pins are withdrawn and the 'runner heads' scooped out (Fig. 8, p. 15). The funnel part is so shaped as to cause the liquid metal to strike downwards upon entering the 'throat'.

The top is now lifted, and 'runners'—or connecting channels —are cut in the mould to connect the pattern with the 'runner pin' holes, to ensure that the molten metal has access to all parts of the mould. These channels are shaped in such a way as to control and confine the flow of the metal, to regulate it, so to speak, in order that it reaches its destination at a certain speed and under a specified condition of flow. The main entrances are round, and if the metal were to travel direct, through a round tunnel, and suddenly meet a fine or thin part of the mould, it can be readily imagined that there might be trouble.

FIG. 8. *Entrance to mould.*

In this case the special connecting tunnel would gradually change from a circular section

through to

The joint is now swept over with a dry brush to make sure that no loose sand remains on the edges of the box. The bellows are then used over the pattern to make quite certain that no dust or parting-sand remains.

The edges of the pattern are slightly damped, and it is tapped here and there to loosen it from the mould, then the pattern is carefully lifted out, leaving its perfect impression in the sand of the mould. Finally, the mould is closed and securely clamped down, ready for casting, which is, perhaps, the most thrilling process connected with pianoforte manufacture.

Casting.

From end to end of the foundry anything from a hundred to two hundred finished moulds lie ready to be filled.

Midway along the building two or three men are anxiously watching the foreman, ready for the word to start. He is running his eye along the lines of boxes and occasionally 'taking a peep' through the small round spy-holes in the cupola, which is a special kind of shaft furnace. It is round in shape and

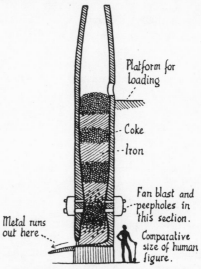

FIG. 9. *Section of the cupola showing method of charging.*

very high; its upper end goes right through the roof into the open air. A very simple sketch is given (Fig. 9), but from within the foundry we can see only the lower part. It is charged from the top, outside the foundry. Just for a moment, let us run up the iron steps to the upper platform, where a workman is charging the cupola. He puts in alternate charges of iron (three parts 'scrap' to one part pig-iron) and coke. The furnace holds about two tons.

Returning below again, the foreman explains that the heat, which is enormous—being in the region of *thirteen hundred and*

The Pianoforte

fifty degrees Centigrade, or thirteen and a half times as hot as boiling water—is generated by means of a blast fan which exerts considerable pressure and drives the air into the furnace itself. Actually, for each pound of coke used, fifteen cubic feet of air-pressure is generated. We can look through one of the special 'peep holes' in the outside wall of the cupola and actually see the molten metal within.

And now everything is ready for 'tapping'. The cupola is really a fearsome object, emitting continually a menacing, muffled roar. Knowing as we do that it is charged with molten iron, we might almost think the contents were determined to break loose.

The 'mouth' of the cupola is really a round hole stopped with clay, which is, of course, quite hard.

A moulder stands ready with a huge 'bogie ladle', which is something like a large copper or saucepan, balanced on two iron wheels, and having a long handle of iron. His ladle is placed just under a spouting which projects from the cupola and guides the metal as it pours from the hole.

The operator takes a long implement and begins to tap the clay which seals the hole in the furnace. The clay begins to crack from the outside edge and the metal pours through the aperture, down the chute, and into the huge bogie ladle.

The heat is intense and the glare almost blinding. Flying sparks of metal, white hot, shoot hissing through the air.[1]

As the ladle begins to fill up, the heat increases in intensity, the glare grows more unbearable. The faces of the moulders, shining with sweat, reflect the orange-coloured light of the molten metal. A workman, with a special kind of shovel, removes the scum which keeps forming on the surface of the metal in the ladle, now nearing its 'safety' capacity.

[1] The writer had a mild shock when a piece of molten metal struck one of the lenses of his spectacles and adhered to it. On examination afterwards it was found that the metal had actually burnt a hole in the surface of the glass. One of the workmen standing near said: 'Good job you had those "specs" on, guv'nor,' and the writer heartily agreed with him.

C   17

The Pianoforte

The furnace-man takes an iron rod having a round metal disk at the end, and fastens a moist and specially prepared clay 'bot' to it; the bot is conical in shape. He carefully takes aim at the hole through which the white-hot metal is still pouring and suddenly rams his rod into it. There are a few stray sparks of flying metal, but almost miraculously the stream is dammed and the flow ceases. The man in charge of the large ladle now wheels it from under the shute and on to a metal track, something like a railway line, to a bay where the moulders stand waiting. Each man carries a hand-ladle on a long iron handle, and one by one they hold their ladles for the metal, which is poured from the larger container.

The glare from the metal, and the heat, must be seen and felt to be fully appreciated. Now the men stand ready round the box or mould, each near an entrance-hole, and when the last man arrives one of them gives the word, and simultaneously they pour the liquid metal into the mould (see frontispiece). At first the metal simply disappears down the apertures, but soon the mould is filled and the holes are full to the very brim. At the same time a series of small explosions occurs and the whole box seems to catch fire. Hundreds of bluish-purple flames are seen to be licking the box and the sand, while clouds of steam are rising into the air. This is the escaping gas burning itself out. From the colour of the flame we might hazard a guess that the gas is largely composed of hydrogen. The flames die down, and amid the steam we can see that the metal in the 'cups' has cooled from whitish-orange to bright red, thence to a dull, angry red, and finally to a very lifeless grey.

Meanwhile the large ladle has supplied all the moulders in the bay, and all round us moulds are being filled and are 'back-firing'; purple flames are discernible through the increasing clouds of steam. The large ladle is now empty and we cannot help following it back to the cupola, to see, a second time, the rather fearsome but very fascinating process of 'tapping'. Once again the cradle runs in, the furnace-man breaks through the clay 'stopper', and the metal pours out. Once again we experience the terrific heat, the blinding glare, the flying sparks, the angry roar of the cupola, and the fierce light on the shining faces of the men. Their skins are now almost black with the sweat and the sand, and the sight is one which we will long retain. There is something fine about these men and something really manly about their work.

And so, the cupola continues to roar, the wheeled ladle comes and goes, the moulders complete their castings, the atmosphere becomes 'thicker', and we feel that there is only one word to describe it—*hectic*. But gradually conditions return to normal, and ultimately the last mould is filled and the spare metal emptied into a prepared mould.

A further surprise awaits us, for the furnace-men now proceed to empty the cupola. They remove the 'floor' and the remains or 'dregs' are allowed to fall out. A number of 'lacework' metal sheets are placed under the cupola, and upon these a huge heap of molten metal, slag, and coke is deposited. The heat is almost unbearable and the fire is slaked by the application of bucket after bucket of water, each of which is greeted, when it meets the metal, by furious hissing and clouds of steam. Soon the molten mass cools down, the glare abates, the men one by one put on their jackets and depart for home.

Next morning, the furnace-men will *enter* the cupola and 'clean it down' ready for recharging. They will prepare another 'clay seal' for the 'mouth' of the furnace, and another spout to guide the liquid metal to the bogie ladle, and while the moulders are completing their fresh moulds others will be preparing the metal for casting.

We must next find out what happens to the newly cast frames. On the following morning the boxes are opened and the frames removed from the moulds. The superfluous sand is swept away, and the 'runners' are knocked off, i.e. the spare metal which does not actually belong to the casting is broken off by being smartly tapped with a hammer.

Each frame is then taken to the sand-blasting machine, which is a very large plant. The frame is really bombarded with fine metal shot and sand, under considerable air pressure. The 'ammunition' is shovelled into a pit at the base of the machine and is conveyed automatically by a moving belt to which buckets are attached. As the belt rotates, the buckets carry the shot to the top of the machine and pour their contents into an enclosed chute or duct. This subdivides and conveys the shot to four nozzles, through which it is driven by means of compressed air. The frame is placed on a moving table, which slides backwards and forwards, and the stream of shot is directed upon it. The frame is then turned upon the table and the reverse side is similarly treated.

The mixture of sand and shot is drawn into the pit, whence it is scooped up by the chain of moving buckets and conveyed once more to the chute at the top of the machine. And so the process is continued.

When the frame is completely freed of sand, it is taken to the trimmer's bench. Here it is 'stoned down' with carborundum 'rubbers' and all surface irregularities are removed.

We must now follow the frame to the machine shop, where first the 'shoulder' is planed on a sliding machine to make sure that it fits exactly to the 'wrest plank' (q.v.). In some frames the metal actually covers the wrest plank, and the 'wrest pins' have to pass through holes in the frame, which are bushed (or lined) with wood, before entering the wrest plank itself. Where this is the case the frame is said to have a 'closed plank', and the holes through the frame have to be bored by machinery.

The 'plank' is marked with a punch by means of a 'jig', which is a template or guide. The drilling machine is very ingenious: a drill constantly revolving can be moved by the operator with ease and rapidity over any spot which is to be drilled, and each operation is completed almost before we have seen it begun. The rest of the 'scale' is marked off with a punch, through an iron template, and drilled.

The 'top treble bridge' is then carefully filed to ensure that the strings lie firmly upon it, so as to make certain that the vibrations of the strings, when mounted, will be absolutely true.

And now, let us watch a workman who seems to 'have a train to catch'. He is driving pins into the holes which have been bored ready to receive them. These pins are cut from a spool of thick wire by a special machine working on the guillotine principle. The workman uses a hammer and a punch which is so made that, when it is placed over the pins which are driven into the holes prepared to receive them, each pin protrudes by exactly the same amount (Fig. 10).

FIG. 10. *Section of a special punch.*

Having driven in all the hitch-pins to the same level, he takes up another punch and proceeds to bend each pin in the same direction, thus making sure that the wires, when mounted, will not slip off the pins (see Fig. 6, p. 9).

The frame is now sprayed with a coat of 'filler' and is then left to dry. The frame is afterwards rubbed down with carborundum paper and frequent applications of water are squeezed from a sponge. Sometimes an automatic rubber is used, consisting of a revolving disk faced with carborundum, but water must be liberally used and the revolutions are very slow, for undue friction would ruin the surface. After the 'undercoating' has been carefully and thoroughly rubbed smooth, the frame is ready for the next and final process.

In the finishing shop two operators are just about to begin. They show us their 'bench', which is a very curious one, for they actually work over a large oblong trough of water. In the centre of the trough is a rectangular 'hopper' which some-

21

how reminds us of the overhanging roof of a Chinese temple. This apparatus is connected with a powerful suction plant, and it draws towards it and through it all the air within its reach. The air must pass downwards towards the surface of the water. There is a special reason for this suction of air which we will better understand in a moment.

The frame is now laid on a fixture, so that it lies over the surface of the water, and the operator takes up an automatic pistol-spray, which has a trigger for controlling the pressure, and a metal cup or container on top.

He pours a cellulose preparation containing bronze into the cup, which has no top, and, pressing the trigger, starts to spray the frame, pointing his pistol slightly downwards. We can smell a faint, sickly odour, something like 'pear-drops'. Gradually the frame begins to gleam in its new coat of gilt, and we notice that the waste cellulose particles are forming a skin on the surface of the water. Immediately they touch it, they 'set'. The suction of the air and the presence of the water have a twofold purpose. They prevent the atomized liquid, which is injurious to health, from entering the lungs of the operators, and enable the waste to be easily and quickly removed.

Where two colours are employed, specially made metal guards are used. The first exposes only that part which is to be green, for example, and the second, when the green is dry, covers it up, leaving the rest to be gilded. The frame, when completely coated, is now left to dry, and is then ready for dispatch to its destination.

We must now go back to the first factory we visited. Here the piano-maker proceeds to screw the frame to the back, *over* the sound-board, and in such a way that the next process, that of stringing, may be carried out.

The wires themselves are known as *strings* and of these several types are used. The short strings, which, as we saw (p. 3), were fixed at the right-hand or treble side of the piano, are single wires, and since they are to produce the high notes they are fairly thin and very short. They are 'bare' wires, i.e. they have no wrapping. It is probably true to say that these strings, of cast steel wire, represent *the strongest elastic material in existence*. We may form some idea of their strength when we realize that a two-foot length of the thinnest wire used (thickness thirteen-and-a-half gauge) would support, without breaking, a weight of something like twenty stone—two hundred and eighty pounds. We ought to realize, too, that all these strings—and there are two hundred and thirty-three in an eighty-eight-note model—remain constantly, for year after year, under enormous tension, without showing any real sign of strain, and this in spite of the fact that, when the dampers are not actually pressing upon them, the hammers are striking them with considerable force.

It is true that a piano, once it has 'settled down', should be tuned at least twice a year, but this very fact in itself proves not only the superb quality of the strings themselves, but also the absolute rigidity of the frame which supports them. It is difficult to arrive at an exact figure which represents the total strain upon a modern instrument, but experts put it in the region of twenty tons, and this, which is a conservative estimate, would mean that an ordinary frame would support, without undue strain, the combined weight of three to four thousand people!

When a string is vibrating, the pitch of the note it produces depends upon three variable quantities, which are inter-dependent, namely, the length, thickness—or density—and the tension—or tightness.

To put it another way, the pitch of a note produced by a string plucked, bowed, or struck, could be raised by making the string thinner—at the same tension and length—or by shortening it, while keeping the other two variants constant, or simply by screwing it up tighter; and the pitch could be lowered by the converse application of these alterations.

To go just a little more into detail, the tension must not be too great, for the vibration might be restricted thereby and the string liable to break. Similarly, the string must not be made too short, for, here again, the vibrations would be impaired and the thickness increased, so that it might become virtually a bar, in which case the vibrations would undergo a complete change.

This explains why the strings producing low notes are wrapped with copper wire, for this has the effect of reducing the vibration rate and so lowering the pitch without extending the length or reducing the tension. It still remains a wire, whereas if a solid wire of equal weight were used it becomes virtually a solid bar, and ceases to vibrate as a string.

At the upper end of the frame the strings are fixed to iron *pegs*. These are the tuning-pegs, which you may have seen the tuner turning when he has come to tune the piano. These pegs are actually driven into the *wrest-plank*, which is part of the back (q.v.). In a good model the wrest-plank consists of a number of layers of hard wood—usually beech—which have been glued together in such a way that the grain of each piece is at right-angles to that on either side of it. This is done to ensure a very tight grip on the peg, which will prevent it from turning under the strain of the string which it carries.

Sometimes the wood of the wrest-plank can be seen, but more usually the pegs, before entering the wood, pass through holes in the iron frame which covers them. The frame-holes are usually bushed with wood, and this helps to prevent the pegs from being bent in the direction of the pull of the string. It may seem strange that iron pegs carrying metal strings are fixed into wooden recesses. The reason is that if the iron peg be tightly screwed into an iron aperture the slightest amount of moisure would cause rust to be deposited between peg and hole, causing the former to jamb and the peg when turned would be liable to snap, leaving a part immovably embedded. Tuning, too, would be very difficult, if not impossible. Many experiments have been tried, without avail, to find a method of mounting the pegs in metal rather than in wood.

Before we can proceed to the actual stringing process, we must have a look at a craftsman who is preparing the bridges which are to carry the strings. He is cutting with a chisel a great number of small bevels on the bridge. These have been very carefully marked beforehand. He then drives in two *bridge-pins* for each wire he is to fix. He black-leads the face surface, left after bevelling, and proceeds with the process of stringing.

The strings themselves are manufactured by another firm, and the wrapped strings, especially, are made in a very interesting way. We will first see some single-wrapped wires being 'spun'. These are 'bi-chord' strings; the core is of steel and the covering of copper wire.

The operator first cuts a suitable length of steel wire—of seventeen gauge for the smallest calibre wrapped string—and proceeds to make the 'eye' or loop at one end. He uses a special pair of patented pliers, having a hole through one of the jaws. He threads one end of the wire through this hole, making a simple loop which he places over a hook fastened to a revolving chuck. He holds the wire tightly in his pliers and starts the machine, which, as it turns, twists the wire to secure the loop. The spare wire is cut off, and the twist completed in one action by closing the pliers at the critical moment. The operator makes 'three-dozen a minute'.

The wire is then taken to a lathe and the loop is put on a hook at one end, while at the other it is fastened round a special contrivance. The wire is then flattened at each end for a distance of perhaps an inch and a half. The reason for this is that this operation prevents the copper wrapping from unwinding again. There are four corners now, which ensure that the coiled wire is fixed.

The lathe—and consequently the wire also, which is stretched between the chucks—revolves very rapidly (11,000 revolutions per minute). The operator now runs a copper wire from a spool, fastens one end to the chuck, and, holding the copper wire and pulling it tight, 'feeds' it through a leather pad which he wears on the palm of his hand, and quickly runs the wire

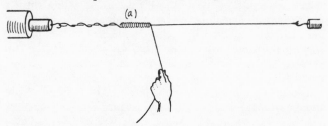

FIG. 11. *The process of wire-spinning.*

along as the revolving core-wire winds the copper covering around it (Fig. 11). It will be noticed from the diagram that the first part of the wrapping is spread out. This is the 'spare': the real wire begins at *a*. This is where the core wire was flattened, and at this point the operator runs the copper wire on tightly, so that there is no space between adjacent coils. He continues to feed the wire until he reaches the other flattened portion of the core-wire. He then cuts the copper wire and stops the lathe. He now cuts off the 'spare' at either end and, starting the lathe again, finishes one end by pressing his pliers, which, like the others we saw, are specially made for the purpose, and are provided with an appliance, against the end of the covering wire as it revolves. He has to be careful here to ensure that the lathe is spinning or revolving in the proper direction, i.e. away from him, or his pliers will unwrap the copper wire. The finish is shown (Fig. 12, p. 27). He now reverses the lathe and 'finishes' the other end of the wire, which he removes from the lathe. It is now ready for use.

In the case of the double-wrapped wires, the first 'spinning' is done as before, but the ends are simply cut, i.e. not finished.

The Pianoforte

Before the second wire is spun, however, the lathe is reversed so that the wire, though wrapped from the same end, is wound in the opposite direction. The spare copper wire at each end is cut off and the ends finished as before.

While we are here we will have a look at the felts and baizes in which this firm also specializes. There are many kinds, which vary greatly in texture, thickness, and colour. The felts are especially interesting, and the mana- ger tells us an interesting story of how its manufacture was first discovered. A monk, apparently, was making a pilgrimage to Canterbury and, having no stockings, placed some raw wool in the soles of his sandals to prevent chafing. After walking many miles, he discovered, on his arrival at Canterbury, that the heat, the moisture, and the friction inside the sandals had 'felted' the wool, and if we were to go to Canterbury to-day we would be able to see felt being made. The secret lies in the fact that each fibre of wool is shaped like the teeth of a saw—this can be verified by the microscope—and is not straight, as one might suppose. The layers of wool are superimposed one upon another in opposite directions, and, under similar but more refined conditions to those which have been described, the strands are 'jockeyed' into position so that they interlock and form a very wonderful and useful material.

FIG. 12. The 'finish' of the wrapped wire (enlarged).

Whereas felt is dependent upon the interlocking of adjacent fibres of wool, baize consists of woven wool, and if we look at a cross-section where it has been cut we can see the woven strands. Both baize and felt are used in the manufacture of the pianoforte, each having its own particular place, according to texture required, but we will see more of this at a later stage.

We must now go back to see how the strings are 'mounted' or fixed to the frame. The steel strings are put on first, for they lie nearest the sound-board. They are received in spools, each of which contains a pound of wire, varying in gauge from 'twenty-two', and diminishing by halves to 'thirteen and a half'.

The operator takes a spool of wire of the requisite gauge and puts the end through the hole in a *wrest-pin*, which has been chalked to ensure that it grips when holding the strain of

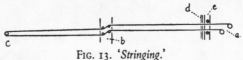

FIG. 13. '*Stringing*.'

a, *Wrest pins*; b, *Bridge pins*; c, *Hitch pin*; d, *Iron bridge of frame*; e, *Pressure-bar*.

the taut wire, while, at the same time, the pin is smooth to turn when the string is being tuned. He places the wrest-pin in a kind of key, such as we have seen piano-tuners use, and turns the wire tightly three or four times round the pin. He then knocks the pin into the wrest-plank, where a hole has been drilled ready to receive it. He runs the wire off the spool, through the bridge-pins, and then round the *hitch-pin* on the frame itself at the far end. He leads the wire back again across the bridge, through the next pair of bridge-pins, making a second or adjacent string, and, having measured and cut the wire, threads this end through the next wrest-pin, turns the wire round it, and drives it into its appropriate hole in the wrest-plank (Fig. 13). When cutting the wire he gauges the requisite length to a nicety, and his judgement is such that when he has threaded his wire through the hole in the second or adjacent wrest-pin, and has turned it round the pin three or four times, the wire on this and on all the other wrest-pins has exactly the same number of turns or coils of wire, and they all 'face' in exactly the same direction (Fig. 14, p. 29).

In the case of the wrapped wires, these have a loop at one end, and this is placed on or over the hitch-pin of the frame, passed through the bridge-pins, as before, cut to the requisite length, threaded through the hole in the wrest-pin, and wound and inserted as were the steel wires.

The Pianoforte

Afterwards, the *pressure-bar* is put on. This is a curved bar of brass (Fig. 15) which is provided at intervals with screw-holes, through which the screws are inserted and driven into the frame. The pressure-bar can be seen on any upright model. You will find it just below the wrest-pins or tuning-pegs, and

FIG. 14. *Wrest-pins and wires.*

FIG. 15. *Section of pressure-bar and screw.*

quite close to the iron bridge of the frame. The real value of the pressure-bar lies in the fact that it puts great pressure on the strings where they make contact with the iron bridge—thus terminating definitely, at the bridge itself, the length of the string which is intended to vibrate.

The strings, having been mounted, are now matched and tuned. This process is known as 'chipping up'. The craftsman tunes the strings and, since the keyboard and action are not yet available, he has to pluck each string with a plectrum made of ivory. Having tuned the whole gamut 'from top to bottom', he proceeds to '*roll*' the strings, using a grooved steel wheel mounted and joined to a handle. He does this to give the strings a thorough stretching, so that they will not sag farther and so lose their pitch. After the rolling process he again 'chips up' or re-tunes the strings as before.

The strings having been mounted and tuned, the embryo pianoforte now goes to the 'fitter-up', as he calls himself: we may, perhaps, think of him as the case-assembler. He receives the various parts of the case partially polished from the polisher. His first job is to fit the *ends*—or sides (see Fig. 16, p. 30). These are glued to the back. The *cheeks* (*b*) are now fitted and glued to the ends. Next, the *bottom-board*, i.e. the

29

base-board, is fixed into position. The *toes* (*h*) are next put in, and the *plinth*, which is the narrow front rail at the foot of the instrument, is now fixed into position.

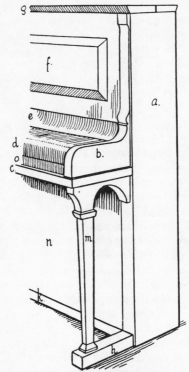

Fig. 16. *The Case components.*

a, *End*; b, *Cheek*; c, *Key-bottom*; d, *Fall*; e, *Hollow*; f, *Top door*; g, *Top*; h, *Toe*; k, *Plinth*; m, *Pillar-support*; n, *Bottom door*; o, *Lock-board.*

The *key-bottom*, which lies under the keys, is then fitted and fixed to the cheeks at either end, but before doing so the 'fitter-up' tells us of two very important measurements to which he has to work. The first is the *strike*. This is the distance from the key-bottom to that point on each wire at which its appropriate hammer will strike it. If the key-bottom be too high, or too low, by even the slightest amount, the hammers will not strike at that point on the strings which the designer intended, and the tone of the instrument will be impaired. The second measurement is known as the *key-bottom measurement*, and fixes the distance from the bridge to the inside face of the lock-board (o). Here again, absolute precision is essential, for on this measurement will depend the distance which the hammer must travel before reaching the string. There is a definite fixed distance for this, and also a definite place in the stroke itself for the point of impact, but we will learn more about this when we visit the action-finisher, who has given these two important measurements to the case-assembler. Where the pianos are intended for export, most of the main joints are both glued and screwed.

The instrument we have been following must now go to the action-finisher's, where we will see it again, and, in order to save time, we will ask to see the complete assembly of another case. When the *lock-board* (o) has been fitted, the *fall and hollow* (d and e) are hinged and placed in position. The fall is that part, usually curved, which covers the keys, and the hollow the piece to which it is hinged.

Next comes the fitting of the *top-door*, which is the trade name for the upper front panel, dowelled ready for insertion. The lower front panel is now fitted, and, finally, the *top*, in two sections and hinged, is fixed to the *back* of the instrument.

'Our' piano has been removed to a department where the keyboard and action will be fitted, but, before seeing it there, we must leave this factory for a while and pay a visit to another manufacturer, who specializes in keyboards and actions.

The *action* is the name given to that part of the piano which actually controls and effects the striking of the strings. For the sake of clarity, the separate mechanism for each note will be referred to as an action-unit, and the various pieces of wood, metal, felt, and so forth, which together constitute a unit, will be called 'parts'.

An action is of no use without its appropriate keyboard: the two are complementary. When the keys are depressed they act as levers, and the ends farthest from the fingers, which are in direct contact with the action, are raised, causing, primarily, the hammer to strike the string and the damper to release it: the latter happens just a fraction of a second before the hammer reaches the string, which is thus free to vibrate.

The importance of the action lies in the fact that the pianist must get his expression or his nuance by the manner in which he strikes the keys, and, equally, by the way in which the action responds to his 'touch'. In a modern instrument the response of keys and action to the touch is almost incredibly delicate, and if you ever go, as you should do, to hear a first-class concert pianist playing on a modern pianoforte you will realize, first, the wonderful technique of the performer and, second, the magnificent response of his instrument.

As we shall see, the action and keyboard are almost entirely machine-made, and here, undoubtedly, this is to be preferred; for the intricate mechanism of the action demands not only great precision in the manufacture of each action-unit and of each part of it, but, also, conformity of every unit with the complete action.

At the outset, it would be well to realize that the mechanical parts of the piano are constructed almost entirely of wood and, since great precision is necessary, the wood itself must be carefully selected and thoroughly seasoned. Both maple, which comes from Canada, and hornbeam, which is imported from France, are used. Each is very hard and of close grain, and is therefore eminently suitable.

We first see the wood in planks, ranging in length from ten to sixteen feet, and of various widths, the narrowest being some six inches wide. These are first sawn into strips, slightly more than two feet long, three inches wide, and an inch and a quarter thick. We see in the yard huge stacks of timber being seasoned.

The strips just mentioned, before entering the factory proper, are seasoned in a very special way, being placed in a huge oven where they are subject to both moisture and heat, each of which can be regulated. After remaining here for some time they are placed in another chamber, where they are subjected to a dry heat. They are then further seasoned in an ordinary atmosphere. The object of all this treatment is to drive out all superfluous sap, which, if allowed to remain, might later 'misbehave' with disastrous results. One can, perhaps, imagine what might happen to a piano if all the hammer shanks were to warp, causing the 'heads' to turn askew; or if other parts were to stick by swelling; or if others, again, were to shrink, causing connexions to come apart.

The strips are now 'shot', i.e. carefully planed, by machinery, on the *edge* faces, and panelled, matched for colour, and glued edge to edge, thus producing a composite board. The board is then cut, planed, first *along* the grain and then *across* it, and 'finished', all this being done by machines. We now see it something like a perfectly finished drawing-board, two feet square by an inch thick, and as smooth as satin.

The board is now cut into strips and moulded, by machines. There are many different shapes, or mouldings, which vary according to the part being made. These strips are then seasoned again for at least six months, to allow them to 'settle down' after the machines have, to some extent, 'upset the grain'.

And now, we will see what happens to a particular strip or moulding. We see it first, as shown (Fig. 17, p. 34). It consists of two separate mouldings, of which the smaller (marked *a*), having been cut, or moulded, by one machine, has been glued into the larger (*b*), which has been moulded by another machine. The moulding as shown (Fig. 17) measures two feet in length by three and a half inches in width. Its thickness can be judged from the sketch.

This strip, together with many others exactly like it, now passes into another department, where it is cut by circular saws into sections (as shown by the dotted line). The operators for this process work very quickly, and since the cut 'slices'

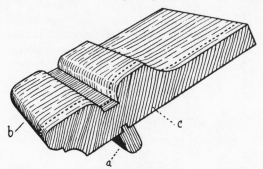

FIG. 17. *Moulding.*

FIG. 18. *Component after leaving the machine.*

are so small they have to be very skilful in picking up each piece as the saw cuts it off, and this with great rapidity. The operator stacks the pieces on trays, which are then conveyed, automatically, to another department, where, in one machine, many separate and distinct processes are carried out. The particular piece in which we are interested enters the machine as at *c* (Fig. 17 above) and, after spending just three seconds within it, emerges as shown (Fig. 18). It is part of the lever (marked *h*, Fig. 19, p. 35). These pieces are being fed into the machine and ejected again in a continuous stream, and

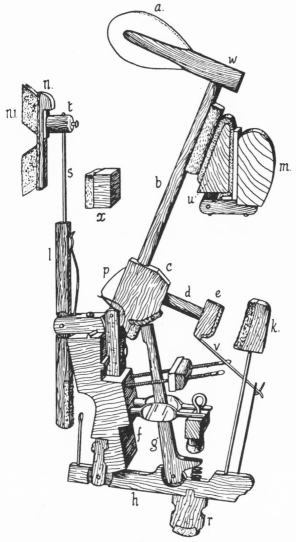

FIG. 19. *Unit of a Pianoforte Action.*

a, *Hammer-head*; b, *Shank*; c, *Butt*; d, *Butt-shank*; e, *Balance hammer-head*;
f, *Beam rail*; g, *Jack*; h, *Lever*; k, *Check-head*; l, *Damper-arm*; m, *Hammer-rest
rail*; n, *Damper-head*; n.1, *Damper*; p, *Hammer-butt spring*; r, *Heel*; s, *Damper-wire*;
t, *Damper-drum*; u, *Hammer-rest*; v, *Check*; w, *Hammer-wood*; x, *Damper slap-
rail*.   (*By permission of Messrs. Herrburger, Brooks, Ltd.*)

there are from twenty-four to thirty pieces—in any one machine—at a time.

In the same way, other moulded strips of many kinds are being treated in a similar fashion. Here, for instance, is another

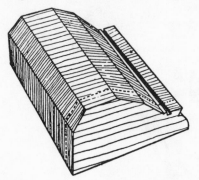

FIG. 20. *Moulding.*   FIG. 21. *Component after leaving the machine.*

strip (Fig. 20), which is first cut into 'slices' (as shown by the dotted line), and these are being 'fed' into the machine which deals with them, and emerge as finished parts (Fig. 21). When all these machines are working there seems to be something inexorable about the whole procedure, and it is a fact that, once a piece of wood begins its journey, there is no turning back; it is, like a cork in a stream, forced to go on and on with the tide.

All these shapes or parts, as they are delivered, are neatly stacked on trays and automatically delivered to the next 'port of call'. It is impossible for us to follow all these processes, and the best we can hope to do is to pick out here and there some particular component and see what happens to it—the *hammer*, for instance.

We first see a number of composite boards, or panels, finished in the same manner as those we saw previously.

These, however, are larger, being four feet square by half an inch thick. They are cut into strips, each three inches wide. Each strip now undergoes a process which is rather difficult to explain; it is moulded and tapered, on both sides, so that it is thicker at one end than the other.

A moulding machine, in the ordinary way, simply turns

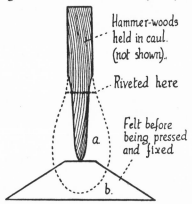

Hammer-woods held in caul. (not shown)..

Riveted here

Felt before being pressed and fixed

a

b.

Press here (not shown).

FIG. 22. *Hammer-head and felt.*

out work of constant or unvarying thickness, and so, to accommodate the strip to the machine-cutting tool, the moulding is placed in a 'buck' or cradle, which is itself tapered. First one side is cut and then the other. The sectional view can be seen (Hammer-wood, Fig. 22).

This tapering is done in such a way that when the strip, which represents a complete set of hammer-heads, or 'hammer-woods', as they are called, is later cut into pieces or strips, these will be graded from one end to the other in size and weight, those destined for the bass hammers being considerably heavier than the treble hammers.

The moulded strips are now cut into pieces three-eighths

of an inch wide and stacked on trays, in sets, and in the relative positions which they occupied before being cut into sections, i.e. tapering from bass to treble.

A complete set is placed in a *caul*, which is a contrivance for keeping the 'heads' close together and in exact alinement while the felt covering is put on. The felt used must be of the finest quality, and great care is exercised by the manufacturer in his choice of material, for inferior felt would ruin the whole action.

The felt is received in sheets, which taper in thickness from one end to the other. These are cut into strips, each of which is tapered and represents a set of felts, corresponding to a set of hammer-woods or 'heads'. The strips are now shaped or moulded as shown (Fig. 22, p. 37), and each is placed in a special hammer-covering press while a set of 'heads' in the caul is placed in position.

The sides of the felt are glued, and the machine put into operation. The action of the press causes the felt 'sides' to be turned round the 'heads', where both remain fixed under pressure (see *a*) until the glue sets, the whole being left in the press for about twelve hours. The 'heads' are later cut into separate units, and riveted through wood and felt to strengthen the join.

We might have wondered why the 'heads' were cut before the felt was affixed. The reason is simply that no tool can cut both. A circular saw would rip the felt, and a knife, while cutting the felt, would be of no use when meeting the hard, close-grained wood of the 'head'. The complete hammer-heads are now *shanked*—the shanks being inserted and glued— and will find their way, ultimately, to the assembly-room, where we hope to see them again.

At *f* (Fig. 19, p. 35) is shown a section of the *beam*. Actually, it runs along the whole extent of the complete action, but has been cut through to show a complete action unit. You will notice that many separate parts are screwed, or otherwise fastened, to it. It is a moulding, and the section is very clearly indicated. It is of quartered maple, by which we mean that the grain is so arranged that the many screws which have to be inserted do not cause it to split.

The part marked *u* is, similarly, a portion of a continuous

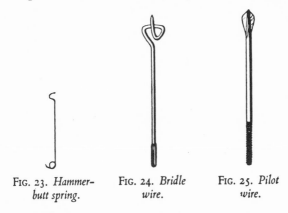

FIG. 23. *Hammer-butt spring.*   FIG. 24. *Bridle wire.*   FIG. 25. *Pilot wire.*

length of wood, which has been cut through to show the unit. It will be noticed that there are numerous metal parts, and these will next engage our attention. The various springs and metal parts of the action are made in a department which we will now visit. Here are several very interesting machines, which are fed from spools with wire of various kinds. Here, for instance, is a machine which cuts the wire into lengths and delivers these as shown (Fig. 23, above). The wire is of brass and as thin as cotton. It is a *hammer-butt spring* and can be seen in position (Fig. 19, p. 35).

Another machine using a much heavier wire is delivering components as shown (Fig. 24); these are *bridle wires*; while a third, consuming a still heavier wire, is ejecting parts which consist of a shaft having a spear-head at one end and being threaded at the other (Fig. 25). These are known as *pilot wires*. All these, and many other parts, each by its destined route, find their way to a large room near the top of the factory and are there assembled and tested by experts.

We now visit the machine-shop, where the machines which do all these wonderful things are themselves made by other machines, and all are actually made on the premises. These may be seen but not described—in any detail.

One cannot help noticing how smoothly, and almost inevitably, all the parts we have seen made, move forward towards their goal—the assembly-room. Some processes naturally take longer than others, but the rate of progress is kept constant by the employment of more 'hands' where the processes are slower, and of fewer operators where they are quicker.

In one shop, for instance, a girl is attending, quite comfortably, six or seven machines simultaneously. These need very little attention and seem almost human in the way in which they look after themselves. In other departments, however, half a dozen operators might be needed on one single process to keep the progression of parts moving smoothly and according to schedule. Perhaps we may best sum it up by quoting the manager's own words: 'The economic conditions are so arranged that, for every given period, a unit is produced.'

And now we finally reach the assembling department, which is a very large and well-lit room. The assemblers are putting together the various parts, of which there are so many that it is impossible to try to understand, or even to see, all that is going on. We notice one line of men who are putting in screws with electrically driven screw-drivers, and here a girl is doing something with pieces of felt, while there another is fastening on tapes. Out of what seems to us to be a hopeless tangle, but which, in reality, is what might be termed an orderly disorder, we see, almost with surprise, complete actions being adjusted and tested by experts, who have graduated by their experience in the various processes which we have described. The actions are now ready for dispatch.

The Pianoforte

Now let us leave the action and see how the *keys* are manufactured. They are made of American bass-wood, which is
white and 'grainless'. It is specially seasoned (see p. 33) and,
after being panelled and planed, each composite board, representing a complete set of keys, is marked out to scale.

The ivories are purchased in the form of elephant tusks and

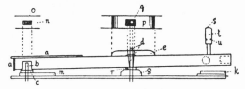

FIG. 26. *Key, cut through vertically.*

a, *Ivory*; b, *Front hole pin*; c, *Felt washer*; d, *Balance pin*; e, *Chase board*;
*f, *Wooden key*; g, *Balance rail*; k, *Felt pad*; m, *Front rail*; n, *Under-view of key,
showing*: o, *Front hole—bushed with felt*; p, *Top-view of chase board, showing*:
q, *Balance-hole—bushed—and pin*; r, *Felt washer*; s, *Connects here with the heel
of the action (see Fig. 19)*; t, *Pilot*; u, *Capstan holes.*

> * [f (wooden key), not included in the diagram, is that part
> to which the ivory (a) and chase board (e) are affixed.]

cut into blocks of specific size before being cut into the strips
which most of us have seen. You will notice on your piano
that all the white keys have two separate pieces of ivory. These
are called 'heads and tails' and are cut in this way to save waste
when cutting. The 'head' is the wide, and the 'tail' the narrow
piece. The small pieces for the ends are similarly cut.

When the ivories are bleached and matched for grain, so that
each head and tail looks like one piece, they are glued to the
composite board or panel in the exact positions which they
are to occupy. The *chase board* is then fixed. This is a strengthening bar which reinforces the key at that point where it has
been bored to take the *balance pin* (see Fig. 26, above).

The whole panel is now bored for the *front* and *balance
holes*. The front hole (Fig. 26) lies over an iron pin on the
front rail of the keyboard and prevents the key from having

too much lateral—i.e. side-to-side—movement. It is intended that the key should move only up and down. The balance holes fit over the iron pins on the *balance rail*: the key, then, is simply a lever, of which the pin is the fulcrum.

The process known as *loading* is rather an important one. Each key is bored near the end farthest from the ivory and is weighted with lead, according to the balance required. In the cheaper instruments, this is done before the panel is cut into separate keys: a groove is cut along the back edge or a transverse hole is bored along the panel (see dotted lines Fig. 26, p. 41) and the aperture filled with lead. For the hand-made models, however, the loading is left to the pianoforte-maker and his experts, each key being loaded separately.

The black keys are not affixed until after the panel has been cut up. The whole panel is now cut into separate keys, an operation which requires a very high degree of skill. It is interesting to note that here the 'ivories' are mounted before the wooden panel is cut, whereas, and for a similar reason, the process was reversed in the case of the hammer-heads, the *wood* being cut first (see pp. 37–38).

The black notes or black keys are made of ebony, which arrives at the factory in billets or logs. These vary in size but average perhaps from six to eight feet in length by a foot in thickness. The wood must be thoroughly seasoned. The ebony pieces are fixed separately, after the keys have been cut from the composite board.

All the keys are now rounded separately and highly finished. They are then assembled and placed upon the key-frame, which has been manufactured and 'pinned' according to the 'scale' of the pianoforte destined to receive them. This is part of the work of the regulator and finisher. He first of all ensures that all keys, both black and white, move freely on both balance and front guiding-pins.

Next, all keys are carefully adjusted and levelled, from bass to treble, to make sure that all the 'whites' and all the 'blacks' are in true alinement and on the same plane. The fact that all the white keys, for example, can be made to present one perfectly flat or level surface has always astonished the writer.

The keyboard and action are now sent to the piano-maker, where you will remember we left the instrument standing ready to receive them; so we will go back to the original factory. The action-finisher is a very skilful craftsman. His work is of vital importance, for he can make or mar the instrument. Just exactly what he does and why would involve a considerable amount of technical detail which hardly enters into the scope of our present study, but in the main his work is very interesting. It will greatly help you to understand the operations he carries out if you have the diagram of the action (Fig. 19, p. 35) handy for reference. The action arrives with the 'section-work', namely, the butts (c), levers (h), and damper-arms (l), screwed to the beam (f).

We have already seen that two important measurements were given to the case-maker or 'fitter-up', namely, the strike and the key-bottom measurement (p. 31). The action-finisher is most particular to see that the action is put into the instrument so as to ensure that the correct distance from the string to the centre of the heel (r) or striking-point of the action is observed.

He then makes sure that the *rake* of the hammers is correct. The rake is the name given to the slope of the hammer-shanks (b) or, in other words, the amount of inclination or variation from the perpendicular. The action itself is screwed to the action-bolts, one of which can be seen at either end of the piano. These are screwed into the wrest-plank, and the rake can be adjusted by varying the extent to which each screw is inserted.

The damper wires (s) are 'cranked' to the strings, i.e. bent in such a way as will bring each damper-drum (t) exactly opposite the strings to be damped and also in alinement. The damper-drums are now in position to receive the dampers (n and n 1), which are adjusted to fit along the direction of the strings, and either glued or screwed, according to the type he is fitting into position.

Next, hammers are fitted: the finisher, by means of a specially marked template—which is something like a ruler—fixes the correct striking points, on the strings, of all the C

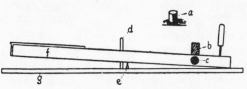

FIG. 27. *Balancing process for loading.*

a, *Lead weight*; b, *Weight in position*; c, *Weight inserted*; d, *Balance pin*; e, *Balance edge*; f, *Key*; 9, *Wooden base of balance tray.*

hammers. He regulates these by cutting each shank to the requisite length. He fixes these in place temporarily and then proceeds to cut, where necessary, all the remaining shanks and insert them. He works with a straight-edge to ensure that each hammer is in perfect alinement, trimming and filing the end of each shank before inserting it. When he is satisfied that all the hammers are in correct position, he glues each shank into its own butt (c), making sure that each hammer-head strikes its corresponding string or strings 'dead true'.

His next job is concerned with the keyboard, and he first shows us how he balances or *loads* each separate key (Fig. 27, above) and why loading is necessary. The keys themselves vary slightly in width, and since the balance-hole position *does not* vary it follows that a certain balance adjustment for each individual key is essential; otherwise, to get an even tone when playing, the pianist would have to vary the pressure on each key according to its state of balance. The keys are loaded then as follows:

The 'loader' takes a single key and places it in position on a balance-tray (see Fig. 27). He then takes a lead weight (*a*) and places it on the key, but nearer to the pin than is shown (*b*). He then gradually moves the lead along until the back end of the key moves downwards, and then marks its position on the side of the key. A hole is bored accordingly and the lead is driven or riveted into it. This completes the loading, and each key goes through the same process.

Although we are not directly concerned with the grand piano, the loading process here is a very interesting one. In this case the action and the hammer work from below the strings, while the damper is above them. The loading is done while the keys are actually in the piano and in contact with the action. The loader, having determined what weight of pressure or 'touch' is needed by the purchaser, uses that weight for each key. Suppose, for example, that a two-ounce pressure is required: he takes a two-ounce weight and places it on a key at that point where the fingers would depress it. He then takes a lead, or perhaps two, and, placing them on the key near the balance-hole, gradually moves them forward, altering first one and then the other—and this time he is moving them towards the *front* of the key—until the front end drops. He then lifts up the key, marks it for boring at the exact places where the leads are, lifts out the key, and inserts the leads as before.

The finisher now shows us how the keys are placed in position. He receives them 'bushed' at the front and balance-holes (see Fig. 26 *o* and *q*, p. 41). He proceeds to put on the felt washers or *balance-pin pads* (*r*), and also the *front-pin pads* (*c*).

The pilots (Fig. 26, p. 41) are now inserted or screwed in and the keys are mounted on the *balance rail* (*g*) in the *key-bed*, each over its appropriate pins and each with its pilot exactly under the corresponding heel (Fig. 19 *r*, p. 35).

Each pilot (Fig. 26 *t*, p. 41) is now adjusted exactly to its heel so that perfect contact between the two is assured, while the hammer-shank lies on the hammer-rest (Fig. 19 *b* and *u*).

The pilot itself is adjusted, in this particular case, on the capstan principle, and the finisher inserts a lever in the capstan-holes and turns the pilot, which is screwed to the pilot-wire, to right or left, until the necessary adjustment is attained, i.e. until there is no loss oᶠ action between pilot and heel. At the same time the hamme must rest, but without actually pressing, upon the rest-rail.

The keys are 'layed' or levelled on the balance-pin pads by adjusting the thickness of each pad, which can be increased by the addition of thin washers. If the pad be too thick, a little of the wood around the balance-hole is planed off. When all the keys are levelled, the depression distance or 'depth of touch' is fixed and regulated in much the same way.

Next comes the process of 'setting-off', the finisher, using a special tool rather like a screw-driver, which has a very long shank, the end being shaped thus: He fits this over the screw on the escapement rail and turns it so as to adjust the hammer-blow in such a way that when the key is *slowly* depressed, the hammer moves without actually striking the string, and stops within a specified distance (e.g. one-eighth of an inch) from it. The dampers are now regulated so that they begin to lift when the hammer, during its stroke and on its way towards the string, is half an inch from its objective.

All the foregoing adjustments require endless time and patience, for each operation has to be done, in a modern pianoforte, *eighty-eight times*! Perhaps you would like to work out how many processes, as far as you have seen, the action-finisher has carried out. He gives the whole work a thorough overhaul, testing and adjusting some slight flaw or variation here and there, and then either tones the instrument or, if another is waiting, has the completed one taken to the 'toner'.

Toning a piano is something akin to 'voicing' an organ pipe. A good toner has to determine by his ear, his only guide, whether each hammer is striking the strings in precisely the right way and at the correct place on the string.

He is now working on the felt of the hammers and is using a strong needle mounted in a holder. Another tool he shows us has four needles mounted in a row and set very close together. He loosens the fibre of the felt by pricking or prodding it with his needle until the correct tone quality for each note, and equality between each and every note, are attained.

He is particularly careful to 'smooth over' the 'breaks'. These are sudden changes of tone between adjacent notes and are liable to occur 'where the bar of the iron frame passes across the bridge, and the latter has to be slotted out'—these are the manager's own words—or where the strings change from triple to duple and from duple to single wires, or from wrapped to unwrapped strings.

Now the toner is matching adjacent notes, playing up and down over a group of semitones, and listening all the time for a note which 'sticks out', as he terms it. When he finds an offender which sounds too hard or too soft, or which does not satisfy him, he sets to work with his needle and makes the necessary adjustment, testing and re-testing note after note until he is satisfied that the tone of each and every note is perfectly attuned.

And so through process after process we have followed the evolution of the piano, and it now stands ready for the case-maker to complete his work, and the polisher, to whom we will now proceed. In this department we can see polish and stains everywhere. The polisher himself is easily distinguished, for his hands and clothes are covered with browny-red. Polishing for pianos must be of a very high standard and lasting quality. The various parts of the case, which are made elsewhere on the premises, come to the polisher in their natural state, but they have already been sand-papered and 'cleaned up'. He first stains the wood, using, as a rule, a water-stain. He next rubs down the surface with fine glass-paper to flatten the grain, which may have been raised by the water. The wood is then 'filled' with a special preparation called a 'stopper' or 'filler', which is rubbed into the surface to stop up the pores. The wood then 'stands' for a day and the filler is 'ground in' (all these are trade terms) with a thin polish and the help of a little pumice powder. Another day is allowed to elapse while this sets or hardens, after which it is 'cut down' or papered with a superfine glass-paper. It is then varnished with shellac spirit varnish and left for two days.

Once again, it is 'cut down' with the same fine paper as was previously used. And now, to use his own words, 'he really begins polishing', and adds a little colour, according to the wood, to tint the polish and 'preserve the colour of the wood', as he puts it. A little raw linseed oil is added as a lubricant, and he rubs on the first coating of polish proper, using a soft pad charged with polish and rubbing gently with a circular motion and paying particular attention to the corners.

The work is then left for a week or so, after which it is again cut down with partly used, superfine glass-paper, or by the use of a special rubber which he calls a 'beaser' or 'beazer'. This consists of a cylinder made of tightly rolled canvas. After a further lapse of time the work is polished again in much the same way as during the last process, and again 'cut down'. All this is part of the main process of '*bodying up*', and each individual constituent process may be described as '*bodying in*'. At this stage the colour-matching of the whole case is perfected, the colour being rubbed in as the polishing is done.

The many parts of the case which we saw at the case-maker's (Fig. 16, p. 30) are now left for a considerable time— often for months—to settle down and thoroughly set.

This is the state in which the fitter-up, who assembles the case, receives them. When the case is partially fitted it goes back to the polisher for a further bodying-up. It then goes to the action-finisher and to the toner, both of whom we have already seen, and returns once more to the polisher. The final polishing is now completed. First the case is polished with 'half-and-half', i.e. half spirit and half polish; this is 'dried out', i.e. polished till the pad is practically dry. Then it is finished off, first with weak benzoin and finally with acid and 'Vienna chalk'. The former brings the oil to the surface and the chalk removes the surplus oil and acid.

And here, at last, is the finished instrument—a fine example of the piano-maker's art.

THE VIOLIN

IT would be very difficult to enter any fiddle-maker's workshop and see an instrument made from beginning to end. For one thing, this would involve many visits, with long periods of waiting in between them, as some of the processes take a considerable time, and during the finishing stages, especially, when the varnishing is being done, each 'coat' must be thoroughly dry before the next can be applied. We are, of course, going to pay a number of visits to the premises of highly skilled craftsmen, but to keep the story 'on the move' it will be supposed that no time has elapsed between successive visits, and also that everything we have seen has been done to one particular fiddle instead of to a number.

The maker will tell you that his instrument is the greatest in the world, and, just between ourselves, if the writer were not also a singer he would be inclined to agree. There is something intimate and personal about a violin which defies description, and an appealing quality about its tone which cannot be analysed. Most musicians would agree that, of all the musical instruments made by man, the violin in the hands of a 'master' not only possesses the most beautiful tone but is capable also of the utmost dexterity.

The greatest violin-makers that the world has yet produced lived some three hundred years ago in the town of Cremona in Italy. In those days violin-making was essentially a family affair, and son followed father in the craft. The first of the great makers which have made Cremona famous were the Amatis, of whom the greatest was Nicolo (1596–1684). Another famous family was that of the Guarnieri, whose most competent member was Giuseppe del Gèsu, and he, perhaps, is the only maker of violins whose work can be said to compare with that of Stradivari (Antonio, 1644–1737), who was the finest craftsman of them all.

The Violin

The instruments which these makers bequeathed to the world have never been surpassed for the perfection of their workmanship, and the beauty of their tone; their age has matured them, and even to-day their designs are still followed by the world's best makers. Countless innovations and experiments have been tried in an endeavour to improve upon the materials and the designs of the Cremona craftsmen, but after nearly three hundred years it cannot be said that any outstanding improvement has been added.

The chief parts which comprise a violin are the body, neck, head, finger-board, tail-piece, bridge, bass-bar, sound-post, and strings. The vibrations produced by the action of the bow are transmitted by the bridge to the body of the instrument, which in turn 'magnifies' the sound: in other words, it acts as a resonator. Both the fabric of the body and the air contained within it are active participants in the sound production. There are many constituent parts, some seventy in all, and most of them are shown here (Fig. 28, p. 52).

The length of the violin is between thirteen and fourteen inches. The upper and lower bouts are curved, partly to strengthen the body of the instrument and also to increase facility in playing. The centre bouts are curved inwards so that the bow may pass from string to string without coming into contact with the sides.

The button holds the shoulder, which is part of the neck, and helps it to resist the strain exerted by the taut strings, which would tend to pull it forward. The arching of the table and back has a dual purpose. It adds greatly to the strength of the body and resists the strain of the strings. It also helps the tone to emerge through the f holes. These are shaped so as to produce the maximum amount of sympathetic vibration on the part of the table.

And now we will visit a well-known modern maker and find out for ourselves something of his art. The workshop seems much smaller and more compact than those which we have previously visited. There is an atmosphere of quietude: no knocking; no machinery; just a handful of men working quietly at their benches, as they might have done three or four

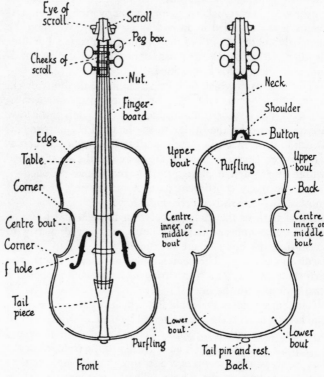

FIG. 28. *Front and back views of the violin.*

hundred years ago. Almost, we feel for the first time like intruders who are breaking a spell. The maker welcomes us, nevertheless, and we begin our tour of inspection.

Everything about us seems so miniature: here on a bench is

an iron plane (Fig. 29) which is only half the length of our thumbs.

On asking to see some raw materials, the maker shows us

FIG. 29. *Oval plane (actual size).*

several slabs of wood of a curious wedge-like shape. They measure roughly sixteen inches by six. Some are of figured maple, others of sycamore. These are destined for the backs of the instruments. The wood comes from the Carpathians, or perhaps from the eastern Alps. He shows us similar pieces of pine, from Switzerland, Germany, or Czechoslovakia, from which the 'belly' or table of the violin will be made. The grain of the pine is perfectly straight, while that of the maple and sycamore is curly.

The method of cutting the slabs is of special interest. The tree is first sawn into logs some sixteen inches in length. The slabs are then cut on the quarter, i.e. from the circumference to the centre of the wood (Fig. 30). Each section is now trimmed and sawn down the middle to within a few inches of the other end (Fig. 31, p. 54). The pieces are not completely separated, and this is a wise precaution, for the two halves which will together form the back are adjacent and will match one another in annual growth and marking. Among innumerable similar pieces, it would be impossible to match them once they had

Section for back.

FIG. 30. *How the slab is cut from the tree.*

'parted company'. The slabs are now stacked to season and to dry thoroughly; they may be stored for five or six years before being used.

It is of interest to note that the maple used by the old

Italian makers was imported from Croatia, Dalmatia, and Turkey. The Turks exported large quantities of the wood to Venice, where it was made into galley-oars. The two nations were generally at war with one another, and the Turks used to select for export to Venice wood which had the greatest number of waves in it, in the hope, no doubt, that oars made from such material would be the more likely to snap when in use.

It was from this 'curly-grained' wood that the old makers selected their raw material. We do not know how much harm may have been done through broken oars, but we *do* know that from this wood the Italian violin-makers constructed hundreds of magnificent instruments whose value to-day would be worth a 'king's ransom'.

The maker first satisfies himself that the wood is thoroughly seasoned. Usually he receives it from a dealer whose material is beyond question. Or he may keep a stock of timber

FIG. 31. *The slab, as the maker actually receives it.*

in reserve to season until such time as he may require it. If the wood is not absolutely dry before being used, the chances are that it will shrink after the violin has been made, and the thicknesses and proportions which may be correct when the instrument leaves the workshop will later, when the wood is further seasoned, shrink and warp in such a way as to render the violin worthless.

Stradivari, like many other makers in Cremona, had an

awning built on the roof of his house where the wood was stored on rafters ready for use.

The maker now separates the slab-backs by completing the cut (Fig. 31, p. 54). He then places the two pieces 'back to back', as shown (Fig. 32). The adjacent edges are 'shot' with a plane, i.e. they are 'trued up' to form a perfect adhesion

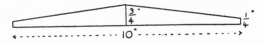

FIG. 32. *How the slab-backs are joined.*

and glued together. The pieces are so arranged that the grain is balanced from the centre symmetrically. The closer grain is near the centre and widens towards the edges. The composite piece (Fig. 32) measures approximately sixteen inches in length. The other measurements are given in the diagram.

The following processes which we are to see may be said to apply to both table and back, the former being made of straight-grained pine, while the latter is generally made of figured maple or sycamore.

The underneath face is now planed level, and on account of the peculiarity of the grain all the cutting and planing must be done *across* the fibre, in the case of figured maple or sycamore. In pine, however, where the grain is straight, the work is done *along* the grain.

A half-pattern template, or pattern of half the table, is now laid on the flat side, and the maker traces round it with a fine pencil. He puts the template with its straight or plain edge exactly along the line of the join made by the two halves of the wood itself. He now turns over the template and traces the corresponding shape on the other half of the wood, thus ensuring perfect symmetry.

The shape just traced is now cut out with a bow-saw, leaving a sixteenth-of-an-inch margin for the saw-marks. (This shape

is called a 'plate' in the trade.) The plate is now carefully cut
with a sharp knife exactly to the marked shape, and is then
finished with a file. The plate is thus complete as far as the
outline or shape is concerned. Next comes a much more
difficult operation, namely, that of modelling, which requires
a high degree of skill and experience. The two faces of the

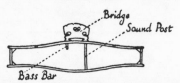

FIG. 33. *Section of the violin, cut across the 'f' holes.*

plate, which are at present quite plain (see sectional view
Fig. 32, p. 55), must be modelled or 'hollowed' until the upper
surface is convex and the lower one concave (Fig. 33).

The maker takes a marking-gauge and 'sets' it carefully to
a specific measurement. He then runs the tool all round the
edge of the plate. The gauge is re-set and a second line is cut
or marked, parallel to the first, the two lines denoting the
thickness of wood which he desires to retain when shaping the
plate. He takes up a gouge, which is a kind of chisel with a
curved cutting-edge, and begins to cut away the surplus wood,
bringing it gradually to the level of the upper gauge-mark all
round the edge. Various gouges are used at different stages
of the cutting.

Our craftsman tells us that he works chiefly 'by instinct' and
his 'eye', but many makers check their modelling by means
of templates. In models fashioned after the Cremona violins
the outer surface of the plate slopes gradually from the highest
point, or summit, to the edges.

As he works, the maker sets out what he describes as his
'long arch', which, if we may borrow a geographical term,
may be described as a watershed running from end to end of

the plate (Fig. 34). Having defined his 'long arch' to some extent, the maker works from various points on the 'long arch' to either edge. Like most good craftsmen, he has improvised many of the tools he uses. One of the planes which violin-makers use is shown, and the illustration depicts the actual

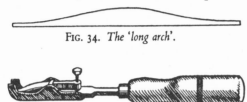

FIG. 34. *The 'long arch'.*

FIG. 35. *Planing tool.*

size (Fig. 29, p. 53). These tend to cramp the fingers, how-ever, and the maker shows us an ingenious adaptation which consists of a plane with a kind of chisel inserted (Fig. 35). Having got this convex face of the plate somewhat to his liking, the maker begins the task of inserting the purfling, a thin strip of wood which serves a dual purpose. It helps to preserve the edges of the model from splintering, by binding or knitting together the fibres, and it also adds greatly to the finished appearance of the instrument. The purfling usually consists of three very thin or narrow strips of wood, usually plane-wood, the outer strips being stained black while the middle strip retains its natural colour. Sometimes they are supplied to the maker already glued together, or they may be inserted separately. The maker, working from the edge and using a special cutting-gauge, makes two deep cuts, parallel to one another, all round it, and with a special 'router' about a sixteenth of an inch in width picks out the wood between the gauge-cuts. Glue is then run into the channel so formed, and the purfling, in six separate lengths, is tapped in gently all round.

The Violin

When the glue has thoroughly set the modelling can be finished off and the purfling slightly hollowed. The sunken part, which is called the gutter, or channel, varies in depth according to the ideas of the designer. Stradivari and Guarnieri models have only slight channels, while those of Amati are considerably deeper. When the 'outside' modelling has been completed the plate is reversed and the inside 'hollowing out' is begun. First the wood is gauged round the edge for the fitting of the ribs or sides of the instrument. It is also marked for the fitting of the end and corner blocks (Fig. 36, p. 59).

As he hollows the plate, the maker must keep a very strict watch on the thickness of it, for this will have a vital effect upon the tone of the fiddle. He works to a thirty-second, and in some cases even to a sixty-fourth, of an inch. He checks the thickness of the wood by means of special callipers (Fig. 37, p. 60). His callipers are an invention of his own and we cannot describe them in detail. We can say, however, that by an ingenious device he can move them all over the plate and read from a moving scale the thickness of the wood he is measuring. He goes into detail about the importance of thickness, which is to some extent subject to the nature and density of the wood. If the plates be too thick the tone will be dull, if too thin the tone will be thin also. Usually the table is slightly thinner than the back. The table tapers in thickness from the middle towards the edges ($\frac{1}{8}$ in. to $\frac{3}{32}$ in.) and thickens again as it approaches the margins beyond the purfling (to $\frac{1}{8}$ in.). The back tapers similarly (from $\frac{5}{32}$ in. to $\frac{3}{32}$ in. at the thinnest part).

These measurements merge into one another imperceptibly, and as the maker cannot see the thickness, he must gauge it from time to time as he works. The back, after being carefully smoothed, is now finished—for the moment, at least.

The front, or table, however, needs further treatment. First the f holes are marked and cut out. The curious shape of these sound-holes is rendered necessary by the arching of the table.

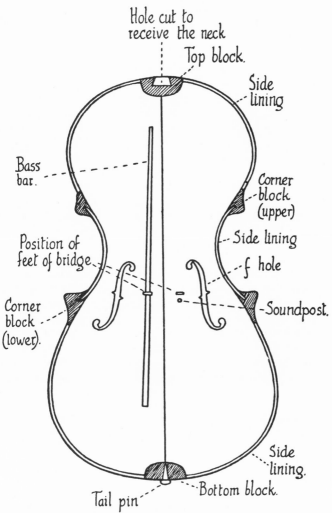

Hole cut to receive the neck

Top block.

Side lining

Bass bar.

Corner block (upper)

Side lining

Position of feet of bridge

f hole

Corner block (lower).

Soundpost.

Side lining.

Tail pin

Bottom block.

FIG. 36. *Details of the construction.*

They really govern the system of vibrations of the whole instrument, and also determine the behaviour of the air contained within the body of the fiddle. They must be accurately cut and must be perfectly symmetrical.

The maker's next job is to fit the bass-bar, or sound-bar. This, together with the sound-post, which we will see later, constitutes what might be termed the nervous system of the

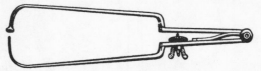

FIG. 37. *Measuring tool.*

violin and consists of a bar of soft pine, about ten and a half inches long. Its exact position is shown (Fig. 36, p. 59). It will be seen that it does not lie exactly parallel to the centre joint. Its width, at the edge glued to the table, is three-sixteenths of an inch, and this edge is curved to conform to the inside of the table to which it is glued. The opposite edge is rounded. Its depth varies, but at its widest part it measures slightly less than half an inch.

When the bridge is later mounted, one of its feet will rest over the bass-bar, while the other will stand almost, but not exactly, over the sound-post. The purpose of the bass-bar is to transmit the vibrations from the strings, via the left foot of the bridge, to the whole of the front plate. It also compensates the effect of cutting the *f* holes, and in addition determines largely the nature of the vibrations themselves. The resonance of the whole fiddle can be regulated by altering the dimensions of the bar.

An interesting fact emerges here, namely, that in many of the world's most famous violins the bass-bars have been too weak for the modern pitch, which is higher than it used to be, and consequently a bar of bigger dimensions is usually substituted for the old one. The operation, however, requires a highly skilled and experienced craftsman.

The table having been completed with *f* holes and sound-

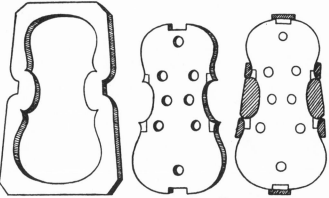

FIG. 38. *Outside mould.*   FIG. 39. *Inside mould.*   FIG. 39a. *Cramping blocks in position.*

bar, we are next shown some strips of figured maple ($\frac{1}{18}$ in. thick by $1\frac{1}{4}$ in. wide) from which the sides or ribs are made. These are first damped and then bent to shape over a hot bending-iron. Sometimes they are cramped, after being bent, on a special mould of hard wood (Figs. 38, 39, and 39a). Sometimes the craftsman, as in this case, simply uses his own judgement and works from the shape of the back which he has just completed.

The four corner-blocks are next

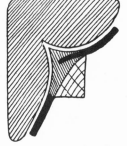

FIG. 40. *Setting the sides, corner-blocks, and side-linings to the moulds.*

cut to shape to receive the ribs, and also to conform to shape with the table and the back (Fig. 40). The linings are

The Violin

then inserted. These are thin strips of pine of section ◿ which are glued all round the inner edges, at top and bottom of the ribs. Their purpose is to strengthen the joint when the back and table are glued to the ribs. They

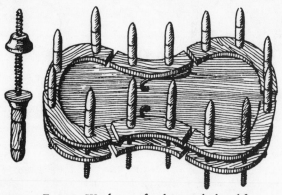

FIG. 41. *Wood cramp for gluing on back and front.*

make a larger surface to be glued, for the ribs themselves are only one-sixteenth of an inch in thickness. They also serve to strengthen the ribs themselves.

The two end blocks are now glued to the ribs and the table and back are glued to the sides, the parts being cramped all round while the glue sets (Fig. 41). Thus the complete body is assembled.

The neck and scroll are made of figured maple or sycamore, and we are shown a block (10 in. by 2½ in.). Templates or patterns are used for marking out the shape on the front and side, and this is cut out with the bow-saw (Fig. 42, p. 63). The carving of the head and scroll is next done, and the recess for the peg is morticed out. The peg-holes are now bored with a special tool, and cleaned out with a reamer. The pegs of ebony or rosewood are then inserted and the finger-board of ebony is glued to the face of the neck. The top nut ensures that the strings just clear the finger-board.

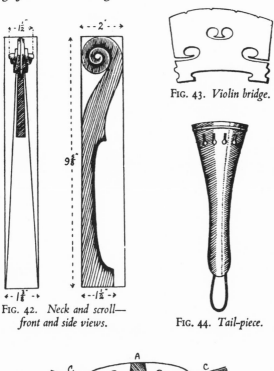

FIG. 43. *Violin bridge.*

FIG. 42. *Neck and scroll— front and side views.*

FIG. 44. *Tail-piece.*

FIG. 45. *Section of tail-pin with sides, side-lining, and block.*
a, *Tail-pin*; b, *Bottom block*; c, *Side lining*; d, *Sides.*

A recess is cut in the top block, and the neck is fitted and glued into it, care being taken to ensure that it lies in a perfectly central position between the *f* holes, and also at the correct elevation for the strings. The position of the neck is carefully checked, first by means of a special template to ensure that the 'rake' or slope is correct, and secondly for perfect alinement with the central joint, from which, by the way, all measurements have been taken, right from the very beginning. This idea of perfect balance or symmetry is of the greatest importance.

The tail-pin (Fig. 45, p. 63) is next put in at the lower end of the fiddle and the small ebony saddle or bottom nut is fitted. The gut which is attached to the tail-piece (Fig. 44, p. 63) is looped round the tail-pin.

The strings are now mounted and the bridge (Fig. 43, p. 63) fitted into position. The importance of the bridge is greater than we might imagine. The shape, including that of the holes, is by no means a question of taste, but is the result of hundreds of years of trial and experiment. It is made of spotted maple, which must be neither too hard nor too soft. The grain should be horizontal, and the bridge should be twice as thick at the base as it is at the top. Its purpose is to transmit the vibrations of the strings to the table, by way of the bass-bar, and to a lesser degree to the back via the sound-post. If it be too thick the transmission of the vibrations of the strings will be retarded. It must not be too low, for this would produce a harsh, piercing tone, nor yet too high, in which case the tone would be dull. So important, indeed, is this factor of height, that the 'lay' of the finger-board when being fitted must be suited to the height of the bridge, and not vice versa. The position of the bridge is shown (Figs. 33 and 36, pp. 56 and 59 respectively).

The sound-post is next inserted. It is simply a little round stick of even-grained pine, about a quarter of an inch in diameter, and of just sufficient length to fit between table and back. When in position it must not be so tight as to exert a strain upon the back and table, for, apart from the distortion of the instrument, the vibrations themselves would be greatly restricted. At the same time it must be sufficiently tight to communicate the vibrations, and also to resist falling out of position when the instrument is knocked or jerked. Its grain must be set at right-angles to that of back and table, otherwise it might tend to 'drive in'.

The exact position of the sound-post is of vital importance in that it affects the tone to a remarkable degree, and its position will depend entirely upon the quality and the peculiarities of the instrument. The maker will probably put it about a quarter of an inch behind the right foot of the bridge and then move it slightly backwards or forwards until he hears the tone he desires. Putting it in, and moving it, is a very delicate operation, for the only means of access is by way of the right-hand *f* hole, and any but an experienced man might be liable to break the hole or damage the interior of the instrument. Special tools are made for this purpose.

And so, at last, the instrument is ready for its final overhaul: strings mounted and tuned, bridge and sound-post in position. Now is the time for corrections and adjustments to be made before the finishing and varnishing are done. When the instrument has finally passed through a searching test, the strings, tail-piece, bridge, and all loose parts are removed, ready for the final finishing and polishing.

The instrument is first 'cleaned up' and smoothed with very fine glass-paper, and is then ready for its first coat of priming. This will form the foundation of the varnish and colouring-matter which will be added subsequently. We have seen how extensively the table and back, particularly, have been cut and gouged, or planed, during the process of modelling. This has left all manner of inequalities of surface grain conditions, and the absorption of varnish by the wood will vary accordingly.

The maker tells us that after long experience he has decided that the best foundation or priming is boiled linseed oil, which is rubbed well into the wood and allowed to dry thoroughly. It fills the pores admirably and ensures drying or setting in readiness for the next process.

F   65

The Violin

The first coat of varnish to be put on will be coloured in accordance with the final shade that has been determined. It will be most probably a yellow or fawn colour. When thoroughly dry this will be rubbed down to eliminate any brush marks or other irregularities (of surface) which may occur. Successive coats of varnish are now applied and each is dried hard before being rubbed down. When the desired depth of shade is reached a final finishing 'coat' is applied, and this must be thoroughly dried and 'hardened out'. It is then 'surfaced down' by the use of the very finest powdered pumice, with the aid of a little boiled linseed oil used as a lubricant. A 'dead mat' surface is the result.

For the final 'finishing off' the maker uses fine Tripoli powder and old linseed oil, which 'brings up', to use his own words, 'a high polished surface'. We cannot leave the subject of varnishing without another reference to the Cremona craftsmen. As a result of their research they discovered the secret of a mixture which was known and used for two hundred years (1550–1750). After the latter date the secret of the ingredients seems to have been lost completely, and it has never been rediscovered.

Antonio Stradivari himself began his varnishing with several coats of oil varnish which contained superfine red gum dissolved in spirit. When the spirit evaporated, the pure gum was left lying on a rich oil varnish. The object of the initial oil varnish which sank into the wood was to show up the grain. Following this a spirit varnish which contained the colouring matter was applied.

The deep red varnish which the Cremona makers applied contained pure 'dragon's blood', which was composed of pure gum in the form of small lumps, like rubies. The yellow varnish used was the unadulterated 'tear' of gamboge. The orange varnish of Guarnieri and Stradivari is simply a mixture of these gums, i.e. 'dragon's blood', exuded from a species of palm fruit, and gamboge, a gum resin obtained from Gambodian and Siamese trees.

66

The Violin

Some experts have averred that the beautiful tone of the Cremona violins was due to their wonderful varnish, but no varnish could make an inferior violin sound well. At the same time it is obvious that the tone of the instrument will be affected to some extent by the final coating which covers and also preserves it. The varnish, even when set thoroughly, must still remain pliant, otherwise the tone will be impaired. It must also be adhesive, or it will crack or peel off.

As a general rule, it may be observed that, in using a well-compounded varnish which is both thin and transparent, at least a dozen separate coats must be applied, each being 'dried out' and rubbed down until the requisite thickness and colour are obtained. As a week, at least, must elapse between the application of successive coats, the time spent on varnishing alone may take from three to four months, and this can be done only on a dry, warm day and in a place which is free from draught.

And now we are shown a finished instrument, a beautiful example, and before taking leave of the maker we ask to hear him play one of his fiddles. Like all good craftsmen, he is proud of his work and anxious that we should share his pleasure.

Our last impression is of him standing on the platform of an empty concert-hall which adjoins the workshop and playing one of his beloved instruments. The beautiful tone which he draws from the strings is an adequate tribute to the care and skill he has expended upon the violin he has made.

BRASS INSTRUMENTS

THERE seems to be something about brass instruments which appeals to the majority of ordinary folk, whether their graceful curves and brilliant polish, or their stirring tones, it would be hard to say, but the fact of their appeal remains. They are, of course, fairly easy to play, and their association with militarism and with uniforms has helped, undoubtedly, to enhance their glamour.

Trumpets, trombones, French horns, and tubas are among the *élite*, being members of the full orchestra, while cornets, euphoniums, tenor horns, and bombardons are regular members of the brass band. All these instruments belong to one great family of which the bugle is perhaps the simplest. The bugler can obtain a series of notes by varying the manner in which he blows or produces them. He does not, and cannot, alter the instrument in any way. Any one of ordinary ability should be able after a few short practices to blow a note on a bugle. By compressing the lips a little more, higher notes can be produced. The usual range obtainable on a B flat bugle is as follows:

In spite of this limited gamut of notes, a skilful bugler can play innumerable tunes, and one has only to think of the military calls such as 'Reveille' or 'The Last Post' to realize how varied and interesting these tunes can be. The notes above are known as harmonics, and any of the brass instruments can produce similar harmonics without being altered in any way. But if the length of the tube and the column of air contained within it is fixed, only the fundamental—or lowest—note, which cannot be produced on all instruments, and the harmonics associated with it, can be obtained.

68

With the keyed instruments, however, such as the trumpet or euphonium, and the slide instruments of which the trombone is the only survivor, the player is able to alter at will, but within certain limits, the length of the air column which is to vibrate, or, to put it another way, the distance which his breath has to travel between mouth-piece and bell, the latter being that part of the instrument from which the air finally emerges. With the trombone, he actually *does* lengthen the instrument, whereas with a valve or keyed model he is able to divert the passage of the breath so as to make it take 'a longer journey', and thus produce a lower note. We will refer to this again at a later stage.

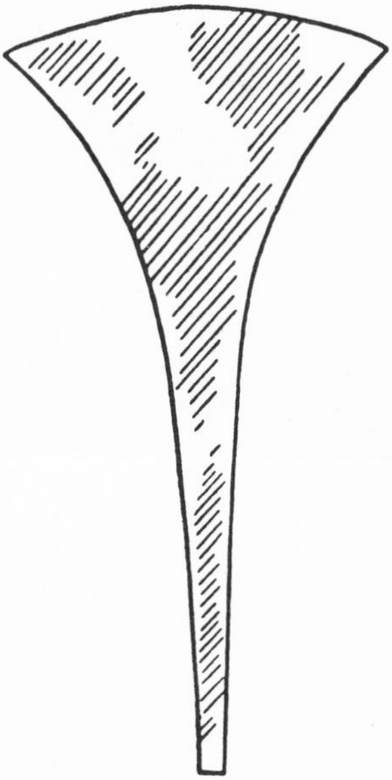

It will be our privilege to visit a large factory where the manufacturer specializes in the making of wind instruments, particularly of brass 'members'.

FIG. 46. *Pattern for a bell section (sheet brass).*

On our arrival we begin our tour by asking the bell-maker to let us see some of his work. He first shows us a master pattern, made of brass (Fig. 46). He lays this on a sheet, also made of brass, upon which he proceeds to trace its shape with a sharp steel 'pencil' or scribe. Then, with a pair of steel shears he cuts out the shape he has traced. He places it on a mandril, which is a 'master shape' of very hard steel (Fig. 47, p. 70), and bends the sheet brass round it, first with his hands and then by beating it with a wooden mallet. Slowly and carefully he continues to shape the metal to the

Brass Instruments

mandril or master pattern until the edges almost meet (Fig. 48). As there is a limit to which the metal may be 'splayed'

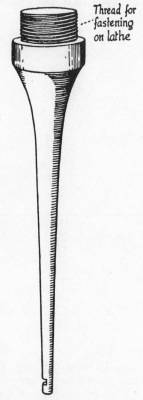

FIG. 47. *Mandril or 'master shape'—of steel.*

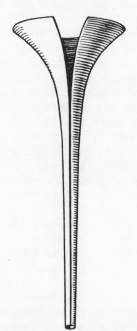

FIG. 48. *Bell section— roughly shaped to the mandril.*

(or stretched out) in the larger instruments, a gusset (Fig. 49, p. 71) is inserted and 'brazed in'.

He removes this roughly shaped funnel from the mandril

70

and carefully beats out or 'splays' the bell end—using an iron pegging-hammer (Fig. 50) and resting it against the rounded edge of a wooden block.

He then beats it again, but this time he places it on a steel

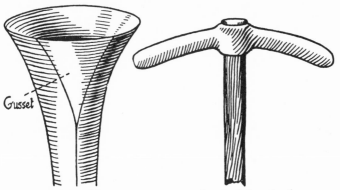

FIG. 49. *Insertion of the gusset.*   FIG. 50. *Iron-headed pegging-hammer.*

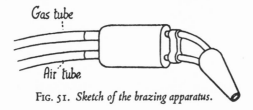

FIG. 51. *Sketch of the brazing apparatus.*

anvil to harden the metal, close up all the pores, and, as he terms it, 'take all the stresses out'. This will prevent 'fire-cracks' during a later process.

The embryo bell is now ready for annealing or softening by heat in the forge. This process must be done very slowly and carefully. The bell-maker uses a twin-fed brazing apparatus burning air and gas; he can regulate the pressure of each so as to vary the proportion of gas to air (Fig. 51 gives a rough idea of the apparatus). He lays the 'bell' on a stout iron pan, packed with lumps of asbestos. The flame plays on the metal, which becomes red hot. When it cools again, we see that the brass has lost its fine yellow brightness and has turned to a dull purple, mottled with ugly orange spots. This, however, is only a temporary state.

The brass is again beaten on the anvil and then goes back to

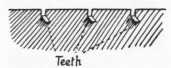

Teeth

FIG. 52. *Sketch showing the teeth.*

the block for further splaying with the pegging hammer. Once more it is hardened on the anvil and taken back to the forge for annealing, thence to the block again for further splaying—or widening—and so the work is continued. Finally the bell, as this, the widest part of the instrument, is called, begins to resemble the shape with which we are familiar.

It is again beaten on the anvil in order to 'knock out the stresses', to quote the bell-maker. Brass is actually an alloy of copper and zinc; the 'stresses' which he distrusts so much are due to the upheaval or upset among the molecules of the metals in the alloy.

Once more it is put upon the mandril, where it is beaten and as nearly joined as possible. Both adjacent edges are now filed in turn, first one and then the other being put outermost simply by running a blade along between the edges.

The bell-maker's next job is to 'stitch up the joint' to keep it in position while he brazes or fuses it.

He takes a pair of pliers which, when used, raises little teeth along one edge (Fig. 52). The other edge is now pushed up against the projecting teeth, which are hammered down, making a very 'handy' fastening which might be likened to 'tacking' in needlework.

When the seam is clipped at intervals from end to end, it is 'painted' or lined with spelter and borax. The former is a film of brass in the form of alloy which has a slightly lower melting-point than brass itself. The borax is used to prevent oxidization.

The bell is now placed on the forge, the blow-lamp is turned on, and the flame begins, once more, to sear the brass; but this time the bell-maker is watching the joint very carefully, plying the flame along the seam, i.e. from end to end.

Soon the metal glows dully. Now it turns a brighter red, growing brighter and hotter until the spelter, almost white hot, begins to run. The moving flame seems to be urging it backwards and forwards, almost in a caressing manner, and then the process suddenly ceases as the operator, at the crucial moment, withdraws the blow-lamp. And as it cools we can see that the heat and the pressure have driven the spelter into the joint, fusing the whole into one inseparable ridge of metal.

The bell is now placed in a 'pickle' of dilute sulphuric acid which will destroy, or nullify, any borax which may persist, for it will have turned hard, like glass, and if allowed to remain would, when hammered, cause pin-holes in the joint.

And so, for a while, we will leave it. The workers are leaving the factory for their mid-day meal, and we, too, are ready for a short 'break'. . . .

On our return, the men are back at work, and here is our bell ready for what further may befall it.

The bell-maker fixes his mandril horizontally in a vice, places the bell on it, and proceeds to hammer it once more along the seam. This process is known as plenishing, that is, beating it down to bring the joint in line with the general thickness of the tube, i.e. to make the joint uniform. A short flat-headed hammer of iron is used for this purpose. The true

roundness of the tube is now restored by beating with a
wooden dresser having a concave face (Fig. 53).

The bell is again further splayed after another annealing at
the forge. Its circumference has now increased by fifty per cent.

Let us ask for the micrometer and measure the thickness of

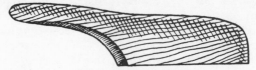

FIG. 53. *Wooden dresser.*

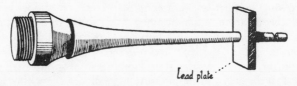

Lead plate

FIG. 54. *Bell—on the mandril—ready to be drawn through the lead plate.*

the brass at the edge of the bell. It shows a decrease of only
three thousandths of an inch, which is hardly as much as we
might have expected.

The bell is now ready for the next process, namely, that of
'drawing', and this is done in another department, to which
we will now proceed. The steel mandril or master-shape is
inserted in the bell until it protrudes at the other end. The
mandril is provided with a niche or catch (Fig. 54) at its
tapered end. The mandril, with the bell upon it, is now
placed on a draw-bench. A clutch is securely fastened to the
mandril and both it and the bell are drawn by the machine
through a hole in a thick lead plate, which is fixed to the
machine in such a way that it cannot move (Fig. 54).

The power exerted by the machine is enormous, and slowly
the steel and its brass casing are pulled through the aperture in

the lead. As the diameter of the metals passing through the lead plate gradually increases, the hole in the lead is stretched, under great strain, so that the aperture always fits exactly, and with extreme pressure, the diameter of the slowly moving tube. The result is that the brass 'covering' is made to fit the

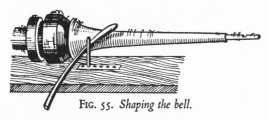

FIG. 55. *Shaping the bell.*

FIG. 56. *Steel burnisher.*

mandril exactly. The tube is 'drawn' until the lead plate is within six inches of the bell—or widest part.

The bell is then removed from the mandril by the drawing machine—in reverse—and both are withdrawn from the machine. The mandril, with the bell upon it, is placed upright on a bench and 'thrown down' several times to ensure that the bell fits the mandril as tightly as possible. The mandril is now placed, horizontally, in a lathe and made to rotate at considerable speed.

The maker then puts a stout steel peg into one of the holes provided on his bench, and with a rounded wooden bar which he uses as a lever he presses the bell hard against the mandril, sweeping the end of his tool outwards towards the widest part of the bell as if he were stroking it, though this 'stroking' is by no means gentle. (The process is shown at Fig. 55.) He now takes a steel burnisher (Fig. 56)

75

with a spatula-shaped end and continues the pressing-out process: the bell is, of course, rotating rapidly on the lathe all the time. The steel burnisher actually closes the 'pores' of the metal and thereby hardens it.

The bell is now ready to be 'spun', that is, to be turned on the lathe and trimmed with a cutting-tool until it is perfectly symmetrical. As soon as the tool starts to pare off the very

FIG. 57. *Edge of the bell
—turned outwards.*   FIG. 58. *Wire inserted.*

thin brass shavings, the metal gleams with its true brightness and at last begins to look like the bell of a trumpet or cornet. The extreme edge is trimmed off with a cutting tool, and another very interesting process is begun.

While the lathe is still rotating, the maker takes another rounded tool and begins to turn the edge of the bell out-wards. He then uses a special pair of pliers, and further turns, or bends, the rim, which is now curved (see Fig. 57). He next cuts off a length of fairly strong wire, and, measuring it carefully, fits it into the groove he has made.

He turns the edge—of the bell—round the wire until it almost completes the circle (Fig. 58). He must not close the joint completely, and we shall see the reason for this in a moment. The next process consists of soft-soldering the joint —and wire—all round the circumference of the bell. The final sealing fixes the wire to the rim of the bell, thereby pre-venting a rattle which might develop when the finished instrument is sounding. This explains why, when enclosing the wire, a tiny space was left whereby the solder could enter. If the joint had been closed up, the solder would have sealed it, but the wire would have been left free to vibrate against the rim enclosing it—a very favourable condition for a constant and annoying rattle.

The bell section is now ready to move once more to

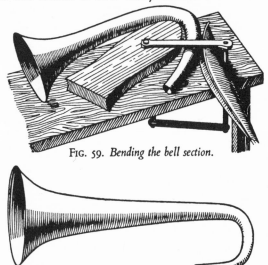

FIG. 59. *Bending the bell section.*

FIG. 60. *Bell section after being bent.*

another department, whither we may accompany it. It must have 'struck' the observant that to bend a tube of thin brass without getting a kink in it is not an easy task, and the method used is very ingenious. The section to be bent is filled with molten lead, which is allowed to cool and solidify. The tube is then slowly turned round a shaped bend (Fig. 59). This is done a little at a time, and between the bending stages the tiny kinks which form are hammered out as they appear. The resultant shape is shown (Fig. 60).

77

When the bending process is complete, the bell is heated until the lead within it is melted—it should be remembered that lead melts at a lower temperature than brass—whereupon the molten lead is poured out again. The smaller parts of the instrument are bent in the same way. While we have been

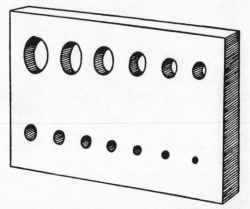

FIG. 61. *Steel draw-plate used for 'diminishing' tube drawing.*

following the evolution of the bell section, other constituent parts of the instrument have been undergoing similar treatment. The various bent sections which we may see in any brass instrument have all been proceeding through one process after another on their way to the assembly room. We have seen that with the lead plate and mandril it was possible to draw a tube of increasing bore. The process can also be applied in the opposite direction: that is to say, a piece of brass tubing can be made smaller and smaller. ─────────── This is accomplished by the use of a steel draw-plate (Fig. 61). The tube to be drawn is knocked, or forced, through holes in the plate, each hole being smaller than the last. Thus the tube is reduced gradually in diameter until the smaller end attains the requisite bore. The tube is then 'fine-drawn' through a lead plate in exactly the same way as we have seen (p. 74).

The larger sections of the instruments are cut from patterns, beaten round mandrils, 'stitched' or 'tacked', brazed, and finished just as was the bell section which we saw.

And now we find ourselves in the assembly-room, a very spacious building, and here all round us are hundreds of parts,

FIG. 62. *Sketch of a 'simplified' trumpet.*

arranged in groups according to the instruments to which they belong.

Before proceeding any farther, however, we are advised to pay a visit to the valve department.

It has already been explained that the valves enable the player to obtain the notes which he wishes to sound. It may now be added that in a brass instrument 'all roads lead' not 'to London' but to the valve section, and this is equally true in the factory. We mentioned the principle on which brass instruments work (p. 68) and it will now be necessary to study in greater detail the function of the valves. Consider for a moment a simple trumpet (Fig. 62) and suppose that we could, if necessary, and while blowing it, make the air—our breath—pass either straight through the trumpet or, alternatively, through each, any, or all the bends as shown. We could, by manipulation, vary the length of the air passage and thereby alter the pitch of the resultant note.

Suppose, for instance, we wished to add to the vibrating column the bend (marked *a*) and the longer bend (marked *c*), we could accomplish this by stopping the air passages as shown.

79

By opening and closing the various sections of tubing we could
divert the air in the following ways:

    1. Straight through the instrument.
    2. Add the *a* bend to 1 above.
    3.   ,,   *b*   ,,   ,,
    4.   ,,   *c*   ,,   ,,
    5.   ,,   *a* and *b* bends to 1 above.
    6.   ,,   *a* and *c*   ,,   ,,
    7.   ,,   *b* and *c*   ,,   ,,
    8.   ,,   *a*, *b*, and *c* bends to 1 above.

The addition of all three bends simultaneously (as at 8
above) represents the longest air passage possible and incidentally the position for the production of the lowest note
obtainable. This is precisely what the valves accomplish. The
instrument is bent several times, and the valves are ingeniously
and compactly arranged in order to economize space and to
facilitate handling and playing, i.e. manipulation. A bombardon, for instance, if 'straightened out', would have a total
length of seven feet four inches. Just imagine yourself march-
ing along the street and *playing it!*

To return to the valves, let us take the trumpet as a typical
example. The notes which lie between the natural harmonics
are obtained by the insertion of three sections of tubing, any
or all of which can be 'added' to the main tube by the use of
valves which close or open the additional sections. The
valves are controlled by three pistons, and any one, any two,
or all three can be used.

The first valve, when the key is depressed and the air diverted
through the extension or *knuckle*, as it is called, adds that length
of tubing which is equivalent to a drop in pitch of a whole
tone; the second valve a semitone, and the third three semitones or a tone and a half.

In all these positions or combinations the trumpet can be
made to produce a different set of natural harmonics on the
fundamental note just as the bugle does in its 'fixed state'.

The construction of a valve is almost too complicated to describe or explain in detail, and yet, since its function is so important, and since also its very complication sets us a problem, why should we not definitely set out to solve and understand it?

If we turn to the sketch (Fig. 63) we will see drawings of a

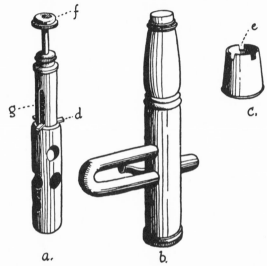

FIG. 63. *Construction of a single valve unit.*

single valve unit. The first picture (*a*) represents the piston. The part marked (*c*) fits inside the outer case (*b*), and the projections (*d*) fit into the slots (*e*). When the piston is de-pressed by the key (*f*) being pushed down, the spring (*g*) is compressed, and when the pressure is released the spring restores the piston to its normal 'up' position.

Now look more carefully at the sectional diagram (Fig. 64, p. 82). When the piston is in its 'up' position (as at I) the air travels straight through the piston, as shown by the arrows. When, however, the piston is depressed (as at II) another 'set of holes' or air passages is brought into play and the air column is diverted through the 'knuckle' or extension, emerging (at *f*); but in this case it has travelled farther before emerging (at *f*) and consequently the resultant note is lowered

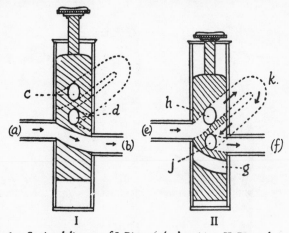

Fig. 64. *Sectional diagram of I. Piston in 'up' position; II. Piston depressed.*
   At I, above. Air passage is a to b. Extension—c to d—closed.
   At II. Air passage is e to h, via k to j and thence to f. Air passage g out of action.
Extension k—open.

in pitch to an extent which will depend upon the length of the section of tubing added.

   The knuckles themselves are loaded with lead and bent by the processes we have already seen. They are afterwards trued up on the inside by the use of a special tool consisting of a steel ball of a size which corresponds to the particular knuckle being made, and this ball is attached to a curved holder (Fig. 65, p. 83). There are many such tools lying about, and it would be difficult to find any two alike, for the balls themselves vary in size, and the 'necks' in shape, according to the curve and bore of the knuckle for which the tool has been made.

The knuckles are then fitted into the holes drilled in the outer casing, and the fit is so exact that even without soldering they look air-tight. The various knuckle-pieces are then inserted and all the joints are silver-soldered by means of a brazier. The process is very similar to that which we saw

FIG. 65. *Special tool used for small bores.*

when the seams were being brazed, but is naturally on a much smaller scale, involving finer and more meticulous work.

The valve section when complete can best be visualized by studying Fig. 66, p. 84.

The projecting tubes which protrude inwards through the outer case are now cut off by means of a tubular saw. This may be described as a hollow steel tube which fits exactly into the outer case and has a toothed or saw edge at one end. When this is affixed to the lathe it cuts off all projections protruding inwards through the outer case.

An inner case is now inserted and soldered into each outer case. A tin—or soft—solder is used. The inside case carries the piston, which is made as a rule of phosphor-bronze in the smaller instruments, while in the larger the pistons are usually made of brass.

The function of the piston and valve has been explained. The fitting of the piston to the inner case involves very accurate measurement and adjustment. The makers work to a thousandth of an inch, for although the piston must slide quite freely in its casing the two must fit so perfectly as to be absolutely air-tight, and not only does this apply to each separate valve but to all three in combination, while at the

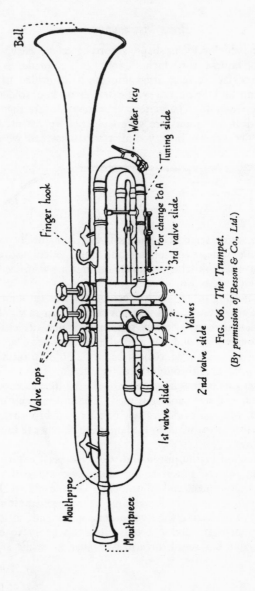

Bell

Water key

Turning slide

Finger hook

for change to A

3rd valve slide

Valve tops

3

2

Valves

1st valve slide

2nd valve slide

Mouthpipe

Mouthpiece

Fig. 66. The Trumpet.
(By permission of Besson & Co., Ltd.)

same time being perfectly free to be depressed at the slightest touch of the fingers.

Our next objective is the assembly-room, where all the various units are being fitted together. It is very difficult to follow the 'evolution' of any particular instrument through all its stages, the reason being that in one department they may be well stocked with certain components and waiting for others. And again, we could hardly expect the whole factory to be thrown out of gear while one particular instrument is completed.

As we look about us we see the men at their benches engaged in piecing together various sections according to the instruments they are assembling. The foreman conducts us to a bench where a bombardon, one of the largest of the brass-band members, has just been assembled. He explains how the sections are connected. Starting from the bell, we find that this section is joined to its adjacent part, the 'large bow', by means of a ferrule which is soft-soldered on. The latter, in turn, is similarly fastened to the 'arm', which is the name given to the adjoining section. The bore of the instrument, with the exception of the valve section, tapers continually from bell to mouthpiece, so that each section we inspect is smaller than the last. Adjoining the arm is the 'small bow', connected as before by a soldered ferrule. The instrument still gradually tapers, and another ferrule connects the small bow with the 'small branch' which carries the tuning slide—a contraption closely resembling a trombone slide in miniature. The 'small branch' leads via a tapered knuckle to the valve section and thence, finally, to the mouthpiece (see Fig. 67, p. 86).

Various stays are fixed, by soldering, between the different sections to strengthen the instrument, and reinforcements or guards are soldered on to parts which are liable to be damaged or dented. Such a guard attached to the 'big bow' is called the 'cap'. The instrument now assembled is passed on to the polisher, who first proceeds to scrape off all surplus

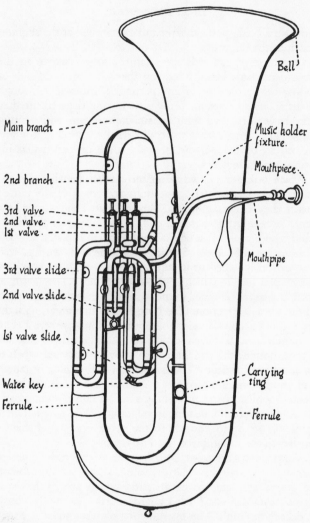

Bell

Main branch

2nd branch

3rd valve
2nd valve
1st valve

3rd valve slide

2nd valve slide

1st valve slide

Water key

Ferrule

Music holder
fixture.

Mouthpiece

Mouthpipe

Carrying
ring

Ferrule

FIG. 67. *The Bombardon.*
(*By permission of Besson & Co., Ltd.*)

solder. Then, with emery-paper and a specially prepared lubricant, he rubs out all surface marks left by the drawing processes or by the mandrils, all hammer-marks on the knuckles, and so forth.

The next process is that of mopping or buffing. Wheels or disks of linen having a brush-like edge are fixed to the lathe and made to revolve at high speed. These take out all marks left by the emery-paper.

The instrument then goes to another department, where the 'listing' is done. This process consists of rubbing by hand with rags dipped in a preparation containing cozal oil and 'rotten stone powder'—which comes from Italy. It is then ready to enter the finisher's department, after which it may be passed out as perfect.

The finisher first polishes the caps. He then ensures that all slides are in perfect working order. Curiously enough, the instrument, during an earlier stage of its growth, may have been mechanically perfect, but subsequent processes or conditions may have caused slight faults to occur—such as a stiff piston—and this may have to be re-ground to fit the inner lining. Corks and springs will also need adjustment. There is usually a cork at either end of each valve, and these, by being either too thin or too thick, may have the effect of bringing the transverse holes through the piston out of alinement with the corresponding passages leading through the holes on the case to the knuckles. The corks prevent noise, or knocking, when the valves are depressed or raised.

Next, the instrument is thoroughly tested to see that it is absolutely air-tight. The foreman, who does this, puts the instrument to his lips and tests the valves individually and in combination by suction on the mouthpipe. Being an expert, he can tell in a moment whether or not each and every valve is functioning properly.

The mouthpiece is now fitted. We are shown a large assortment of mouthpieces and see them first as castings just as they have left the moulds. They are put on the lathe, where the cup and rim are turned. Each instrument has, of course, its own particular mouthpiece, and these vary greatly in size and shape, and are not interchangeable. The mouthpiece is now bored and afterwards shaped with a tapered reamer. That part which is to be inserted is turned and tapered to fit into the mouth-pipe. The length which protrudes, when firmly fitted, is of great importance, as it definitely affects the pitch of the instrument, according to the amount it adds to the length of the instrument.

One of the last and most important processes is that performed by the engraver who cuts in the brass those inscriptions and designs which add so much to the appearance of the finished article. Here is the engraver—and designer—working on the bell of a completed instrument, which he rests on a cloth pad. He first marks out with a steel point a design of flowers and leaves. He then takes a narrow, sharp cutting-tool and very skilfully cuts out the pattern. He seems very quick and sure as he works, although if he were to make a mistake the instrument might be ruined, and it may be worth anything up to fifty pounds! The final process takes place in the tuners' room, where experts will test the tone and intonation of the instrument and also definitely fix its pitch, which latter is of vital importance, for the pitch must conform with that of the other 'members' of the band to which the instrument is assigned.

The tuners' room and their work are described in detail in the section dealing with wood-wind (q.v.). Most of the work we have seen in this factory has been done by hand, but we will now visit another firm where brass instruments are made but where the machine is much more in evidence. The processes are very interesting but quite different from what we have just seen. The method employed is known as *deep drawing*, and it is used in the manufacture of millions of articles of the tin-plate variety.

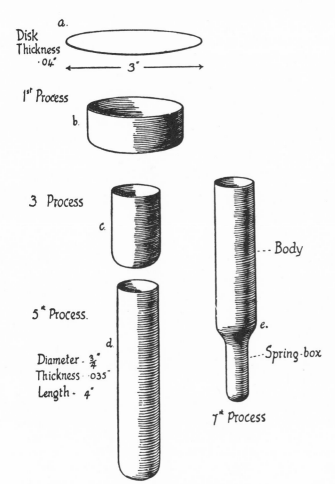

Disk
Thickness
·04˝

a.

←——— 3˝ ———→

1st Process

b.

3 Process

c.

5ᵗ Process.

Diameter · ¾˝
Thickness · 035˝
Length · 4˝

d.

----- Body

e.

---- Spring-box

7ᵗ Process

FIG. 68. *Evolution of a piston.*

The time at our disposal does not permit a full and detailed description of each and every process, so we must content ourselves with a brief outline of the manufacture of one or two component parts. Let us see some of the machines which are doing this work. To begin with, we are shown a metal disk (Fig. 68 *a*, p. 89) destined to become a piston, which, as we have seen, is a component of the valve. The disk measures three inches in diameter and is about four-hundredths of an

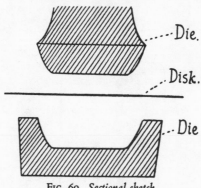

FIG. 69. *Sectional sketch.*

inch thick. It is placed in a compressing machine which exerts an enormous pressure. A lever is moved, the compressor descends, and on its being raised again we find that the disk has been stamped into the form of a shallow cup (*b*). We cannot, of course, see the inside of the machine, but it seems obvious that the disk has been pressed between two dies, one which we might call the 'positive' and the other the 'negative'. A rough sketch (Fig. 69) will give an idea of what we imagine might happen to the plate. When the upper die descends with great pressure upon the lower we can conceive that the disk will be pressed between them and assume the shape defined by the space between the dies.

The 'cup' now goes to another machine of a similar type

and is again compressed, being ejected this time as a deeper cup of smaller diameter (Fig. 68 *c*). Again it moves on and is further compressed. In five processes the disk has become a cylinder four inches in length by three-quarters in diameter (*d*). There is no joint, of course, nor is there any sign of a crack or flaw in the metal. This seems incredible, but it may be explained that between processes the metal is annealed or made malleable by heat to counteract its hardening and to restore the molecular equilibrium to which reference has already been made. On measuring the thickness of the cylinder (*d*), we are somewhat surprised to find that this has diminished by only one two-hundredth part of an inch (i.e. from 0·04 in. to 0·035 in.).

In all, there are seven or eight processes, some of which are shown. The final shape is depicted (at *e*) where the spring-box has been drawn. This component will now go on to another department, where it will be finished on the lathe.

And now let us look at a much larger job. We see, first, a brass disk measuring ten and three-quarter inches in diameter. It is destined to become the bell-section of a baritone saxophone (Fig. 70, p. 92). The disk is placed on the 'table' of a very powerful machine, the lever is operated, and the compressor descends. On its being raised again, we see that the disk has assumed the shape of a soup-plate (*b*). We follow it to another machine, which further alters its shape to that of a shallow cup (*c*). In five separate operations, with annealing processes in between, the plate becomes a cylinder closed at one end (*d*) and measuring thirteen inches in length by three in diameter. But the most astonishing processes of all now await us. We are shown a steel mould in two separate halves and of great strength.

Two such moulds are shown (Fig. 71 *a* and *b*, p. 93). In these sketches it has been supposed that the blocks are transparent so that the mould can be seen within. We now approach another machine which we are told develops enormous power. The first mould (Fig. 71 *a*) is placed on the bed of this machine, is clamped down and fixed into position. The closed end of the brass cylinder we have been watching

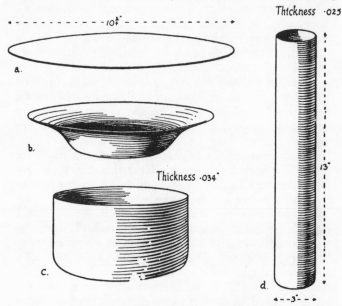

FIG. 70. *Evolution of a baritone saxophone bell.*
(*This is continued in* Figs. 71 *and* 72.)

is placed within the entrance to the mould and a horizontal steel piston is placed within the open end of the cylinder projecting from the mould. The piston itself is actually a very stout tube and water at enormous pressure (*one and a half tons to the square inch*) can be projected through it, and into the brass cylinder, by the machine. We are warned to 'stand back, in case of accidents', and especially on account of the tremendous hydraulic pressure being exerted. A lever is operated and the rod moves forward, pushing the cylinder into the mould, while at the same time the hydraulic pressure

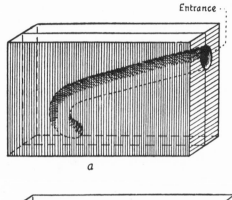

Entrance

a

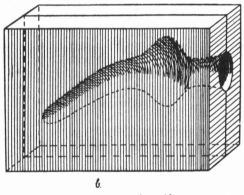

b

FIG. 71. *Typical moulds.*

[*Note: the upper mould is not the actual one described in the text, but is similar to it.*]

is released. The process only takes a moment; the pressure is shut off and the rod withdrawn. When the mould is opened we can see that the cylinder has been forced into the

93

mould and round the bend. Confined by the walls of the mould on its outer surface, and under tremendous pressure on its inner side, the brass has had no option but to assume the shape assigned to it.

The next process is, if anything, even more remarkable, and the machine larger and more powerful. This time the mould

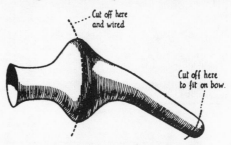

FIG. 72. *Further stage of saxophone bell.*

(shown in Fig. 71 *b*, p. 93) is used. It is clamped down on the 'bed', as before, and again we are specially warned not to get too near. The bent cylinder is once more placed into position, the hollow piston moves forward, and we hear the hiss of the escaping water as it pours from the mould and flows away by the channel designed to receive it. The water itself is milky and contains certain chemicals which assist the process. When the mould is taken apart and the shape removed we find that it has been blown out into a veritable brass bubble and has assumed the exact shape of the mould.

It will now be cut through as shown (Fig. 72) and the edge will be turned and wired, as we saw (p. 76).

Before leaving this factory we may ask just why the deep drawing and hydraulic processes are used. The reason is partly that in the bell we have just seen there is no join whatever, and also that once the machines are installed increased production is facilitated. It is not possible, however, to make the narrower bells such as those of the trumpet, cornet, and bugle, for there is a limit beyond which deep-drawing cannot go, and the bells just mentioned are still made by the older hand process.

But from time to time new innovations are tested and, when satisfactory, incorporated; new machines and improvements are devised. A modern factory such as this 'never stands still'

WOOD-WIND

OUR next visit will be to a large modern factory where we shall be shown something of the manufacture of wood-wind instruments. Of these, the piccolo and flute are pure wind instruments, the sound being produced by blowing across a hole. Clarinets have a single reed, while oboes, English horns, bassoons, and double-bassoons are each provided with 'a pair' of reeds. The instruments named above are placed in increasing order of size and descending order of pitch. The piccolo is the smallest and has the highest 'voice', while the double-bassoon, sometimes called the contra-bassoon, is the largest of the group and has also the deepest tone. It corresponds with the tuba or bombardon in the bass group, the double-bass of the strings, and the timpani of the percussion section. All are very large instruments with very low 'voices'.

Whereas with the brass members the pitch of the various notes is obtained by the gradual or systematic lengthening of the vibrating air column, with the wood-wind the reverse holds good and the column is shortened.

It may be said that, other things being equal, the longer the tube which produces a note the lower will be the note produced. If the tube be provided with holes placed at certain intervals along it, and if all these be closed or covered, the uncovering of the hole farthest from the vibrating agent will have the same effect upon the pitch as if the tube had been sawn off at that point at which the hole occurs. As each additional hole is uncovered, the tube becomes virtually shorter and produces a correspondingly higher note. By this method of shortening the air column the player has in one instrument the equivalent of many pipes of different lengths. This, briefly, is the principle upon which all wood-wind instruments work.

Now try to obtain a tin whistle or flageolet. Put the mouthpiece between your lips and hold the whistle with both hands so that the first, second, and third fingers of the left hand are covering the first, second, and third holes—counting from the mouthpiece—while the corresponding fingers of the right hand are covering the three remaining holes. Make sure that all holes are completely closed. Now blow the whistle and listen to the note. Next, lift the finger farthest from the mouthpiece, i.e. the third finger of the right hand, and blow again. The second note will be a tone higher than the first. Raise the middle finger of the right hand so that only four holes remain covered. The resultant note will be again a tone higher than the last. Continue to remove one finger at a time until all the holes are open and you will find that you are playing up the diatonic scale. The top note or upper tonic—some of you may know it as the 'top doh'—is obtained by covering all the holes except that which is nearest the mouthpiece. If you try 'going up the scale' again you will find that by blowing harder you can obtain harmonics or upper notes usually an octave higher than the lower notes.

The whistle or flageolet shows very simply the system upon which all wood-wind instruments are founded. For thousands of years musicians and craftsmen have experimented with wind instruments, improving the fingering by mechanical contrivances and introducing levers, keys, and so forth. Modern instruments such as the clarinet and oboe are very intricate models, but they all work on modifications or developments of the six-hole 'shortening' system.

Let us now visit a factory, where on arrival we see a fine, modern, well-lit group of buildings. The manager is expecting us and immediately we begin our tour. We ask to see some raw material. Here in a large shed are a number of logs—of African blackwood,—'as hard as iron', about a foot thick, and cut into lengths varying from five to six feet. We ask why they are cut to this particular length and the manager's reply is rather a surprising one: 'Because that length represents the limit of what two men can carry on their heads.' The wood apparently grows in the tropical swamps of Africa and the native carriers transport the logs to the nearest station, or collecting post and 'dump' them. Here they lie until they are collected for shipment.

The carriers usually have a stick with a fork at one end. When they wish to unload the burden from their heads they first place their sticks upright and lower their bodies until the log rests in the two forks. Both log and rests are then pushed outwards and fall to the ground clear of the carriers. A good specimen log weighs from two to two and a half hundred-weight.

The logs pass to another department where they are sawn through into sections of varying lengths according to the size of the parts of the instruments required. The segments are then split along the grain and roughly hewn into rounded shapes, both the splitting and the shaping being done by hand with choppers. We see various heaps of these roughly modelled pieces lying about. Many have been condemned and the wastage seems enormous. The slightest crack, knot, or flaw is fatal, for these pieces are destined to be made into the barrels or tubes of flutes, oboes, and the like. When mentioning the small percentage of pieces which are passed as suitable the manager replies, 'Oh yes, the waste is appalling. In fact, if we get ten pounds of suitable wood from every two hundredweight we reckon we are doing pretty well.'

'Is this the only material you can use, then?'

'Oh no! We use a fair amount of cocus-wood (a very hard brownish wood that comes from the West Indies), and, of course, there's ebonite, which is very hard and durable, and good stuff to work.'

'Does the material affect the tone-quality at all?' we ask.

'Well, personally, I doubt very much whether it matters if the material be wood, ebonite, or metal, so long as the instrument is well made. But musicians, you know, are very particular, and like the rest of us they have their fads and fancies. Some will have nothing but wood, others go for ebonite, or metal, and so we have to please them all.'

But let us pass into the next department, where the selected pieces are roughly turned on the lathe and bored to facilitate seasoning. They are stacked inside the building and afterwards are soaked in oil for six weeks or so; the harder the wood the longer it takes to soak. These sections, which are known as

FIG. 73. *Bassoon joint.*

'joints', are then left so that the oil may dry, and those of cocus wood are placed in strong light to colour, when they turn a deep, golden brown.

All these turned pieces of wood are seasoned for as long a time as the maker can spare. They are strung in sets, like beads, on cords, and suspended from hooks on the walls of the room. Some, we notice, have two borings through them. These are bassoon joints and the double bore is explained by the fact that in the bassoon the air column is doubled back upon itself for the sake of convenience in handling, or, to put it another way, it

is constructed on the hair-pin principle, thus (

(Fig. 73). We notice that these particular sections are much lighter in colour than those destined for the smaller instruments. Some are of rosewood, which is 'reddish' in colour, and these are used for the French type of bassoon, while others of maple or sycamore are used for the German type. Here, too, we see the various bell sections, roughly turned and bored, being seasoned in the same way. There are many sizes and shapes here, each representing some section or other of the various instruments of the wood-wind fraternity.

And now for a little while we will follow the adventures of one particular joint. Here is one, perfectly seasoned, turned, and ready to go on. The joint is first marked with a drill, very carefully and with great precision, for the boring of the holes in the tube, some of which will later be opened or closed for the production of the notes of the scale; others, much smaller, into which the pillars bearing the levers will be screwed.

The machine which does the actual boring is so arranged that the tube or joint is fixed horizontally to a movable table while the drill itself remains fixed above. The joint can be so manipulated that any spot can be brought directly under the drill, and it can also be rotated so that any point on its circumference can be bored, and this can be done either perpendicularly or obliquely through the tube. We have explained that the pillar-holes are much smaller than the air-holes, but even these latter vary in size. For each type of hole to be bored a special drill is inserted in the machine. That which makes the peg-holes, for example, cuts at the same time the crowns which will receive and fit exactly against the peg.

Before passing on, let us examine for a moment some of these tools, which are called 'reamers'. Where an instrument such as the oboe has a bore which gradually increases in size, or tapers, the inside of the barrel is first drilled to a cylindrical or parallel bore. It is then reamered on a lathe with a specially made tapered cutting-tool. The reamers, each of such a size as will fit the instrument for which it is intended, resemble tapered steels such as are sometimes used for sharpening knives, though these reamers are usually much longer (Fig. 74, p. 101) and have a groove cut in them as shown. One of the edges, which protrudes by a fractional amount, is very sharp indeed. As the tool revolves and is pressed into the bore it tapers it to precisely the required shape.

Meanwhile, what has been happening to the joint which we

were following? Here it is, and one of the craftsmen is waiting at his bench ready to show us how a 'key' is mounted.
The craftsman first threads two adjacent key-holes, using a
small tool which is designed to put a thread on the plain bore

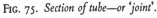

FIG. 74. *Reamer.*

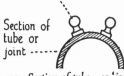

FIG. 75. *Section of tube—or 'joint'.*   FIG. 76. *Mounting a key.*

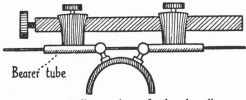

FIG. 77. *Drilling appliance fixed to the pillars.*

left by the machine. He now screws in two small pillars (Fig.
75), making sure that these are of the right size, for some
keys require shorter pillars than others. Having screwed them
in, he must drill through the heads—a rather difficult job, as far
as we can see. First of all, how can he drill straight through
from A to B (Fig. 76) and be sure of getting perfect alinement? His answer to this is complete and convincing.

He takes up another tool, not very large but perfect in
every detail. If we can recall it, perhaps the accompany-
ing sketch will help to make it clearer (Fig. 77). Having

adjusted the tool in position ready for the drilling process, he screws up the bearer tubes until they grip the balls of the pillars, and then, with a long, fine drill working on the lathe and directed for alinement by the tubes on the instrument, he drills a hole through each ball, one from either end.

He then shows us another and very interesting process, namely, making a barrel and soldering it to a key. Even on

FIG. 78. *Simple key.*

one instrument, many different kinds of keys are mounted. Some close holes which normally are open, others uncover holes which are usually shut. One of the simplest types of key is shown (Fig. 78). Such a key is found on the flute. The mounter, as he is called, takes a key and, placing the cup exactly over the hole it is to cover or close, makes a mark on the metal at that point which lies exactly between the heads of the pillars he has just inserted. Next, he cuts off a length of very fine tubing for the barrel. He now proceeds to file a round hole through the key, which when completed exactly fits the barrel which he pushes through the aperture he has made. It fits exactly—so tightly, indeed, that it could not be shaken out. He now 'paints' the joint with flux and with a miniature blow-pipe silver-solders the joint. The barrel is firmly attached to the key, which is placed between the pillars bored to receive it, and a tiny barrel-screw is passed through one pillar-head and screwed into the other. This work requires absolute precision, both in measurement and execution, and yet the mounter does it so quickly and so cleverly as to make the task appear easy. Key-mounting, you can see, has to be done by experts.

Wood-Wind

Many keys of different shape and size are similarly mounted, until the joint seems to be loaded to its utmost capacity. Then the inner joints or 'tenons' are covered by being wrapped with waxed hemp, or with cork, as the case may be, and bands, i.e. metal ferrules, are fitted to the outer joints to prevent cracking when the instrument is assembled and later when it is in use.

The bands are cut on a lathe from a length of tubing and put on in some cases, as we have said, to prevent the outer joint from cracking or splitting, and in others to protect the instrument against wear and rough handling.

We must now visit another expert, whose job it is to clean up or 'true up' the inside bore. This is one of the most important processes of all, for upon the condition of the finished bore will depend, largely, the tone quality of the completed model. Here again we are shown two very efficient tools which are used on the lathe. They are so much alike as to appear identical. Each consists of a solid steel cylinder about a foot in length and of a diameter corresponding to that of the joint to be treated. At either end is a guide which extends for a third of the total length; the guides are perfectly round and fit exactly into the joint now being made. The middle section is also cylindrical but is provided with a cutting-edge which protrudes so little that it increases the diameter of the existing bore by only one thousandth part of an inch. This is passed through the joint. The second tool is of such a diameter that the guides are exactly the size of the cutter, on the first tool, while the cutter again is a thousandth of an inch larger in diameter. The second cutting-tool is also passed through the bore, which is tested with steel gauges, and these register the minutest disparity.

The bore is then glass-papered on the lathe and finally polished with a rod having a cloth wrapping smeared with a special composition of what is known as lustre soap.

Pads are now fitted to the keys. The pads consist of a layer of cardboard and one of felt and are covered with white kid. The caps are slightly heated and the pads fitted by means of an adhesive. Springs are fitted to keys, and keys to pillars. Keys are warmed again and pressed firmly, to ensure the exact fitting of coverings to holes.

Before proceeding to the assembling department we should

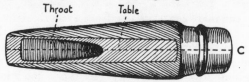

FIG. 79. *Clarinet mouthpiece.*

FIG. 80. *Sectional view of mouthpiece, sawn through the centre.*

perhaps pay a visit to the mouthpiece maker. The mouthpiece is an important part of any wood-wind model, as it affects both the tone and pitch of the instrument. It is usually made of ebonite, as this best withstands the effect of moisture from the mouth. Here is a craftsman who is actually modelling a mouthpiece for a clarinet. He tells us that the job on which he is working was first turned on the lathe and then 'flattened' on one side for the bed or table on which, later, the reed will lie: straightforward work, though it needs care and precision. This man's job is somewhat more difficult, for he has to cut out or model the 'throat', which is the air-passage through it, and his work may almost be described as tunnelling in miniature. The cutting must all be done by hand, and the illustrations (Figs. 79, 80) will give some idea of what has to be done.

104

The drawing shows the aperture through which, when made, the craftsman must work. The tunnel emerges again at *C*. The sketch (Fig. 80, p. 104) gives the sectional view of the mouthpiece when sawn through along the dotted line, the

FIG. 81. *Special tool used for mouthpiece.*

shaded portion indicating the chamber which is actually hollowed out by the maker. It will be seen that to a large extent he is, to use his own phrase 'working in the dark'. In other words, he cannot actually see what he is doing, and uses gauges to guide him. The first is what he terms a 'slot' gauge. He lays this on the table and by means of it marks out the shape of what we might call the 'entrance to the tunnel'.

FIG. 82. *Special tool used for mouth-piece.*

He begins to bore his way downwards into the solid ebonite, using a set of tools which we have never seen before and which he tells us he has made as the need has arisen. He refers to them as 'primitive', but to us the word hardly seems a suitable one. Some are like files with curved cutting-edges (Fig. 81), while others resemble modifications of wood-carvers' tools (Fig. 82).

As he hollows out the channel or 'throat' he uses another gauge (Fig. 83, p. 106). This is called a 'profile', or 'gullet-gauge'. And so with file and cutter and careful checkings with various gauges he completes the operation.

The instrument is next assembled with socket, mouthpiece, joint, and bell, and is ready for the testing of mechanical parts and to ensure that joint fittings are in perfect order and pads absolutely air-tight. Each instrument must have the mouthpiece originally made especially for it and must be tested as a complete whole. We saw a moment ago how the mouthpiece was fashioned, and mention was made (p. 104) of the table and reed. The latter is a most important item, for its vibrations actually produce the sound, which is then modified by the instrument. The reed is to the wood-wind player what

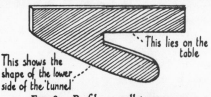

This lies on the table

This shows the shape of the lower side of the 'tunnel'

FIG. 83. *Profile, or gullet gauge.*

the fly is to the fisherman: it is a personal thing having an intangible individuality about it which is hard to define. Expert players select and treat their reeds with very great care and usually trim them to suit their own peculiar requirements.

On visiting the reed-maker's department we ask first about the materials from which they are made. He thereupon shows us some lengths of a particular kind of cane which is specially chosen for its resilience or springiness. It resembles bamboo but is much superior for reed-making purposes, and we are told that it is imported from southern Spain and from the Var Valley in France.

The canes themselves are hollow and they vary in length from four to ten inches. They are obviously sections cut between the knots which, of course, have been removed. They vary somewhat in diameter but average perhaps nearly an inch across, while the thickness of the wood itself may be anything from one to three-eighths of an inch. They are graded in size according to the instruments for which they are destined, namely, all the clarinets from the 'A' or 'B flat' to the 'bass', and the saxophones from the 'soprano' to the baritone 'sax'—i.e. from the smallest to the largest.

Wood-Wind

The reed-maker selects a length of cane suitable for the particular reed he is making and to which his machines are 'set'. He takes it to a bench whereon is a curious cane-splitting device. It consists of a central iron rod fixed to a heavy round metal base and having four steel cutting-blades fixed near the upper end of the bar. The blades are set at right-angles and resemble the flights on a metal dart (see Fig. 84). The maker presses the cane down upon the cutters and knocks it with a wooden mallet, whereupon it is split length-wise into four quarter sections (Fig. 87 a, p. 111).

FIG. 84. *Cane splitter.*

These he cuts into the requisite lengths on a miniature circular saw having an adjustable guide which is pre-set to ensure that the cut portions are of the exact length required.

The next process is the planing of the hollow side of the pieces. In order to do this he places a piece of cane with its inner surface uppermost on a metal sliding table, having a special spring-clamp to hold the wood in place. By means of a lever the table is then moved so that it slides under a revolving table, which has a number of steel cutters projecting downwards. This revolves at high speed, and as it is pressed downwards it pares off the superfluous cane, leaving the upper face flat (Fig. 87 b, p. 111).

The cane is now placed in the trimming machine, which has two sliding chisel-edged cutters, and these remove the edges of the cane, leaving it the exact width (see Fig. 87 c). The cane is now placed on the table of another machine (see Fig. 85, p. 108) for fine planing. The planing tool is hinged and

107

can be raised and lowered. It is attached to a metal rod which in turn is connected to a small fly-wheel, and this when it revolves causes the plane to move backwards and forwards like a shuttle. When the cane is in position the cutter is

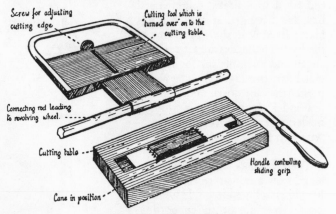

FIG. 85. *Fine-planing machine.*

lowered and gently pressed down upon it. The machine then completes the planing of the flat or inner surface.

We must now go to a somewhat complicated machine which actually shapes the cane into a reed, and the maker calls it the blade-shaping machine. It consists of two main parts, one above the other. Below there are three separate units (Fig. 86 *a*, *b*, pp. 109, 110) which are so connected in parallel that when the middle one is rotated the other two move by exactly the same amount. Thus all three are always at exactly the same angle or deviation from the perpendicular (see Fig. 86 *a*). The unit on either side is an iron block to which is screwed a steel master-shape or matrix. Between them there is another block on the top of which is a 'table', and on this the reed, inverted, is secured by a special clamp. The reed now has its curved or outside surface uppermost. An arm projecting downwards, can be moved or rotated by the operator. Above this there is a somewhat complicated planing arrangement which has on either side a steel roller which rests on its corresponding

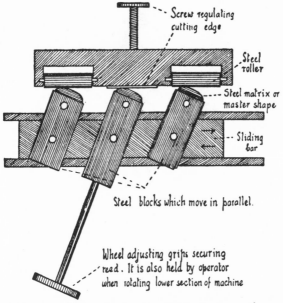

Fig. 86 a. *Section of main parts of blade-shaping machine.*

steel pattern. The central unit is a plane, carefully adjusted, and this pares off the superfluous wood. The plane moves shuttlewise along the direction of the cane, and when this has been secured the machine is started and the operator, by slowly moving the arm, gradually turns the table from one side to the other. The two outer blocks bearing the steel patterns move to exactly the same degree, so that as the plane moves backward and forward, the operator lightly presses

109

Wood-Wind

it down with one hand, while guiding the movement of the table—and reed—with the other, the cane begins to assume the exact shape of the 'master'-pattern on either side of it.

When the reed is removed we find that it has been shaped

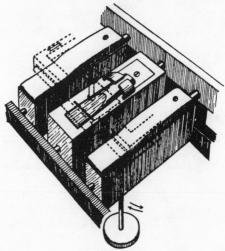

FIG. 86 b. *Drawing of blade-shaping machine showing—in dotted lines— the cutter superimposed.*

and tapered at one end to a fine edge as thin as paper. The reed is then 'filed square' (Fig. 87 d) by hand, and finally the thin end is trimmed by means of a shaped cutter acting on the guillotine principle operated by a lever which lowers the cutting-blade (Fig. 87 e).

The reed is now finished and is ready to be screwed into position on the table of the mouthpiece.

The whole time taken for all the processes we have just seen would not occupy much more than five minutes, and the reed-maker tells us that he makes on an average about a thousand reeds in a week.

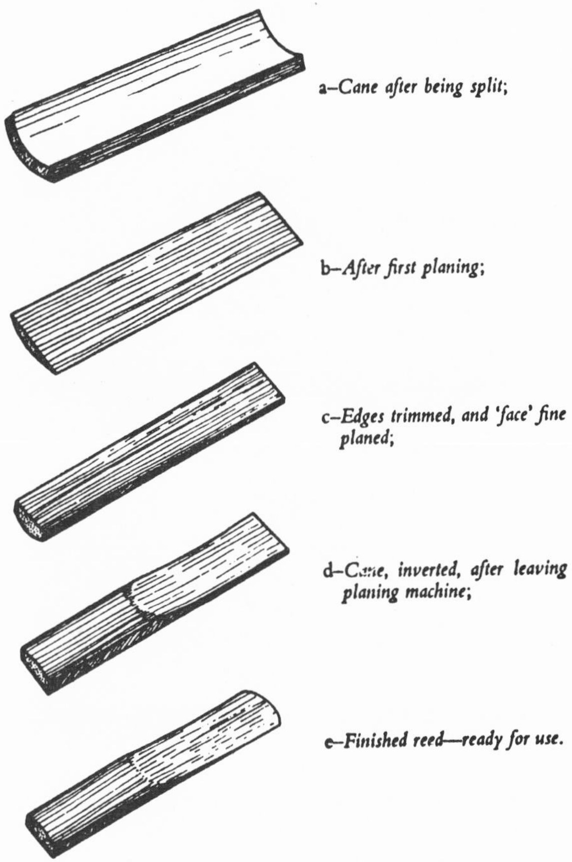

a—*Cane after being split;*

b—*After first planing;*

c—*Edges trimmed, and 'face' fine
planed;*

d—*Cane, inverted, after leaving
planing machine;*

e—*Finished reed—ready for use.*

FIG. 87. *Evolution of a clarinet reed.*

It is now ready for the tuner and we must pay him a visit,
for he is a very important person and will probably have
many interesting things to tell us. The tuner's department is
a bright and cheerful room. Ranged round the walls on

shelves are many kinds of wind instruments, most of which are newly made and ready for final tuning. There are two experts here, one for the brass and the other for the wood-wind members.

On one wall there are many 'tuning boxes' or tuning units, each consisting of a metal bar mounted in such a way as to be free to vibrate when struck with a rubber-headed hammer. Behind the bar to which it is attached is an oblong wooden box with a large hole on the face side and lying under the metal bar. The box itself acts as a resonator and intensifies the sound made by the bar when struck. Each tuning-box is marked showing the number of vibrations per second. On this number or frequency, as it is called, depends the pitch of the note, and there are several different standards of pitch.

In one corner of the room is an organ having four stops, each of which is marked with a different vibration number, and each represents a complete range of notes, which can be operated from the one keyboard. The tuners have an expert knowledge of their subject and we will ask them how they carry out their task. They tell us that first the pitch of a note is determined by the rate of vibration of whatever agent is producing the note, and second that the vibrations double in frequency for each octave rise in the pitch. Thirdly, two notes of slightly different pitch when sounded together will create a dissonance; that is, they will sound discordant, harsh, or 'unfriendly'.

This dissonance will set up a beat, and the curious thing about this beat is that it occurs regularly, a certain number of times per second, and this number is precisely the same as the difference between the vibration rates of the two notes previously mentioned.

Here is a simple example. The organ plays the A above middle C, say at 435 vibrations per second. Another instrument now plays the same A but at the rate of 438 vibrations. The frequency of the latter note is three more per second than the former, and the beats are heard quite plainly three times per second. If both notes were raised in pitch by an exact octave the beats would occur *six* times every second, and so forth.

But here a difficulty presents itself: the vibration rate of a musical note increases with the rise of temperature, so that an instrument tuned at 50 degrees Fahrenheit and then played in a room at 70 degrees would be definitely out of tune. The rise, particularly in the region of 'tuning A' (i.e. the note to which we hear the instruments tuning before the start of an orchestral concert) is two vibrations per second for every ten degrees rise in temperature.

A moment ago we were talking about the beat, i.e. the dissonance beat. Suppose a customer asks the tuners to prepare a set of instruments for a hot country where the temperature might often rise, for example, to ninety or even a hundred degrees. Suppose also that the lowest tuning stop on this special tuning organ is A = 435 at 60 degrees and the client wants his instrument tuned to A = 431 at 60 degrees.

The tuner pulls out his 435 stop and begins to tune the A of the instrument. At first he makes a shrewd guess, but later by the aid of a stop-watch he begins to tune more carefully. He cannot blow the instrument he is tuning for much longer than ten or fifteen seconds at a time, and so he adopts a ten or fifteen second interval, both of which are exact divisions of a minute, as his tuning unit. When the beat to which he has been listening occurs exactly four times per second he knows that the pitch vibration is exactly 431 per second. He knows also that the frequency when affected by the heat will give the particular pitch desired.

There is one further point of interest which ought to be mentioned. In an orchestra, and when the room becomes heated, one section gets flatter while the other two tend to sharpen. The pitch of the strings drops slightly, but these are easily tuned again. The brass and the wood-wind tend to

I

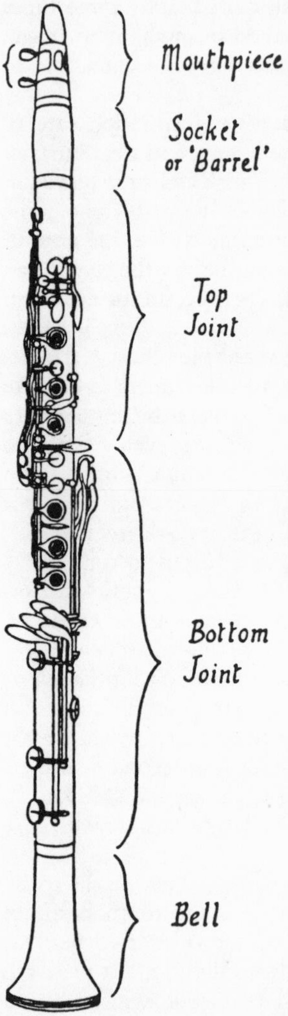

Mouthpiece

Socket
or 'Barrel'

Top
Joint

Bottom
Joint

Bell

rise and are accordingly fitted with tuning-slides which can be adjusted to compensate for this.

Before leaving the tuner's room we will ask the wood-wind expert to run over briefly the procedure he adopts when passing an instrument as satisfactory. He first tests the model for tone-quality and freedom of production. If the instrument is 'awkward' to manipulate or tends to produce 'false notes', or if the tone is unduly weak or lacking in quality, he will suspect the presence of a faulty joint or an ill-fitting pad and return the instrument to the workshop, though he hastens to assure us that such an occurrence is very rare indeed.

Before actually tuning an instrument he 'warms it up' by blowing through it for a while to raise it to normal concert-hall temperature (i.e. 68 degrees F.). If he were to tune the instrument while it is cold it would be appreciably out of tune when played under concert conditions.

He carefully tests each note, comparing it with the standard

Fig. 88. *Improved Boehm Clarinet (by permission of Boosey & Hawkes, Ltd., London)*.

equivalent on the organ, listening for the beat which would proclaim a disparity in pitch, and playing all the time in the 'centre of the note', as he terms it. He mentions one interesting fact, namely, that tuners must be very careful to resist the temptation to humour a note. By this he means that a good player can, by altering the embouchure—i.e. the manner in which he grips the reed or mouthpiece with his lips—definitely raise or lower the pitch of any particular note. With a competent performer this process of humouring becomes almost instinctive.

Finally, when the model has undergone the most searching scrutiny both for performance and appearance, it is ready for packing and dispatch (see Fig. 88).

ORGAN

THE organ, in its present form, is a miracle of ingenuity and craftsmanship representing the accumulation of centuries of experiment. It is a wind instrument, the sound being produced by pipes which are made to 'speak' through air pressure, known as 'wind'. The pitch is controlled by the player from the keyboards, operated by the hands, and also from the pedals, which are played by the feet; the tone is varied by the manipulation of stops which when in use permit the wind to enter those ranks of pipes which are required to sound.

The wind is generated by compression, the air being drawn into a bellows, or pressure generator and then forced by means of one-way valves into a kind of reservoir (see Fig. 115, p.156). (Here is shown a modern multiple fan generator.) In the older organs large bellows driven by hand or hydraulic power were used. In the reservoir the wind-pressure is kept constant by a system which need not be described at the moment. From the reservoir it proceeds by way of an air-pipe—known as a wind trunk—to a wind-chest on which the pipes are situated.

In order to understand how the wind finally gains access to the particular pipes which are intended to sound, it is necessary to return to the keyboard and draw-knobs. When the organist presses down a key on one of the manuals—which is the proper name for the keyboards—the pallet connected with that key is opened so that the wind can pass through the grid by way of the channel to the underside of the sound-board, i.e. to the table. (This is clearly shown in Figs. 104–108, pp. 142–3, where the technical names of the parts just mentioned, and of others, may be studied.) Before the wind can proceed any farther, however, the organist must put 'on' a stop. In other words, he must pull out a draw-knob or operate a thumb or toe piston which causes the slide (see Fig. 106) to

116

move into such a position that the holes in the slide are exactly over those in the table. Thus the wind is allowed to make its way through the slide to the upper board and thence into the pipe, causing it to 'speak' or sound.

The mechanical contrivances connecting a draw-knob with

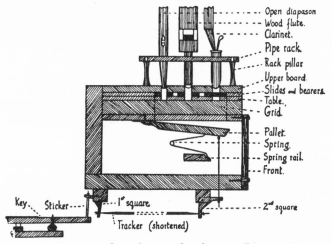

FIG. 89. *Mechanical action—key down—pallet open.*

its corresponding slide are similar to those between the key and pallet (Figs. 89, above, 90, p. 118, and 112, p. 153) and need not therefore be described in detail. Similarly, 'coupling' is effected on much the same principle; but the word itself may be explained. Let us suppose that an organist plays a note, say middle 'C', on one of the manuals. By operating certain 'couplers'—or coupling draw-knobs—and without depressing any additional keys he can also cause the 'C' an octave above or an octave below to sound; or he might couple the note he is playing with the corresponding note or notes on other manuals. By this means he is able to play

117

combinations of notes, both in pitch and in tone colour, which his fingers, unaided, could never accomplish.

One main section of the organ is the *console* or keyboard section where the organist sits with his keyboards, called manuals, his draw-knobs, and the various devices for hands

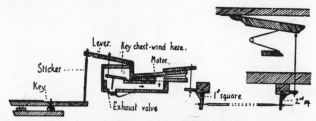

FIG. 90. *Early form of pneumatic action operating first square, tracker, second square, and pallet.*

and feet within easy reach. All control originates from the console (which is described in detail on p. 129).

Another section is the *action* where the operations of the organist at the console are translated into terms of mechanical action. Thirdly, there is the *pipe* section where the sound is produced and the intentions of the organist fulfilled. With the pipes should be included the *wind supply*. Since the action and pipes are usually placed close together, we might consider the entire instrument as consisting of console, action—including the pipes—and wind supply.

We shall find that the organs in general use throughout this country may be divided into three main groups. In the oldest, which are termed *mechanical*, all movements of keys, draw-knobs—or pistons—volume control, and so forth are controlled by direct mechanical action in the form of levers, 'stickers', and 'squares' (see Fig. 89, p. 117). Organ-builders and players found such actions both cumbersome and unwieldy. The combined efforts of ingenious experimenters, however, led to the introduction of *pneumatic action*, in which air pressure was used to actuate levers and stops by means of what are termed *motors*. These consist of bellows of various sizes which when inflated—or deflated—do the work of the older levers and rods (Fig. 90, p. 118, and also Fig. 112, p. 153). Since they receive their motive power from the wind supply and not directly through the pressure of the organist's fingers or feet, they save the performer much physical exertion, and indeed their inception was an event of supreme importance.

The all-pneumatic system, though a great improvement on the mechanical action above mentioned, had several drawbacks, of which we need mention only one. Where the distance between the keys and the pipes was considerable, there was loss of time between the pressing of the key and the ensuing sound, although in the best pneumatic actions the response was practically instantaneous at a distance of anything up to sixty feet. Electricity, which has invaded so many fields, has solved this problem of 'delayed' action over longer distances, and in the modern *electric-pneumatic* action the impulses made on the console are conveyed electrically (from the console) by means of contacts which complete electrical circuits and thus operate electro-magnets (see Fig. 115, p. 156). These in turn control the motors, to which reference has been made. The motors open the pallets in the wind chest and so the pipes are made to speak. Thus the distance between console and pipes has been bridged electrically in such a way that complete synchronization is attained and response is practically instantaneous.

In a large church or concert-hall organ the sum total of parts runs into many hundreds of thousands and the cost may be as much as £20,000. Such an instrument costing this sum of money was being installed, at the time of writing, in Westminster Abbey.

We are not surprised to find, on visiting an organ factory for the first time, that we have entered a very large establishment. Let us begin by inspecting the timber-yard where the

Organ

wood is stored to season. There seems to be enough timber here to build a hundred organs. We are shown British Columbian pine, Canadian whitewood, sequoia from Western Canada and Siberia, mahogany from Honduras, cedar from Borneo, English oak, and oak from Austria and Japan, and teak from Burma. All this timber is stacked under cover but open to the air and consequently to atmospheric changes. Most of it has already been kiln-dried and is now being stored for further seasoning under natural conditions.

As we would like to take a closer look at some of this timber, the foreman shows us first some British Columbian pine, which some of us may know as Douglas fir. It is a very strong wood of light colour and good even grain. It is used in the building of the interior framework of the organ. The boards vary in size and measure from two to three inches in thickness, from six to twelve inches in width, and in length anything from twenty to thirty feet.

Douglas firs often attain heights of two hundred and fifty feet and exceed five feet in diameter. The gigantic flagstaff at Kew Gardens, London, which was presented to this country by the Canadian Government, is of Douglas fir. It measures two hundred and sixteen feet in length and from end to end there is neither flaw nor defect.

We come next to some cedar, which the foreman tells us is a very 'straight' or 'dead' wood. To use his own words, 'it doesn't move—i.e. warp or twist—once it's on a job.' He asks us to smell it, and we note its pleasing odour, which, by the way, is a protection against insect pests. This particular consignment comes from British Honduras. And here is some Western pine. The boards are whitish yellow in colour and of great size, some measuring thirty-four feet by four and varying in thickness from one inch to two inches. The grain is wonderfully straight. This kind of wood is therefore used for the making of sound-boards (upon which the pipes stand) because it does not warp or twist.

Organ

Farther on we come to some very interesting timber. It is sequoia and somewhat resembles cedar, being of light brown colour. Some of these boards are of enormous size. In length they often run to forty feet and even greater lengths are obtainable. In width they measure as much as five or six feet, and boards of this great size are practically free from knot or flaw of any kind. The wood is chiefly used for the construction of the larger wooden pipes, the largest of which are thirty-two feet in length. Before leaving this sequoia wood perhaps a word about the trees themselves may be of interest. They grow to an enormous size, sometimes towering four hundred feet into the air and measuring as much as ninety feet in circumference at the base. As a general rule their age ranges from four hundred to fifteen hundred years, but some of the very largest are estimated to be between four and five thousand years old. Actually the largest of these trees, which grow on the slopes of the Sierra Nevada in California, are the oldest living things on earth, and there are living specimens here which may have been alive when the Egyptians were building the pyramids.

Some of the finest wood used for organ work comes from Canada. This pale, cream-coloured wood, for instance, is Canadian Western pine which is used for the finer work, while next to it lies some Siberian pine of coarser texture which we are told is used for the 'rougher work'.

Here is timber we can all recognize—mahogany. This is from Honduras and is of perfectly straight grain. These are very fine boards indeed, some twenty feet in length and half a yard wide, varying in thickness from one inch to three inches. Organ-builders like the straight-grained variety because it does not warp. Now we are shown another wood which we have not seen before. It is Borneo cedar, and our guide describes it as a 'mild' wood which is used for magnet-boards. He tells us that it must 'stand' after being worked upon—i.e. drilling, &c.

Red birch, which we are next shown, is very fine and hard. It is of Canadian origin and is used for the pedals and similar parts which are liable to hard wear. Here, too, is oak from various sources. Figured oak is used for case work for consoles, panels, and the like. The best figured variety is reserved for draw-stop jambs, and for console and case work, panels, and similar parts which show, and where their appearance must be considered.

Probably one of the most serviceable woods in general use is teak. It is impervious to the action of water and also to a less extent to fire. For the latter reason the London County Council has ordained that all 'units' shall be cased in teak—within the London area. Some firms encase their actions and pipe-sections in asbestos, but teak is in general use for this purpose. It is brown, very close-grained, resembles mahogany in some ways, and comes from Burma.

Finally we are shown a varied selection of ply-wood. Here, for instance, is some birch-ply, oak-faced. It is in boards, some of which are five feet, others six feet, by four feet in width, and each board contains eleven or twelve separate layers of wood. It is not possible to see all the raw material, or the thousands of component parts that go to make up a modern organ, but we can just ask our guide to show us the store. In a large factory such as this everything needed for the manufacture of the organ is kept in stock, and many of the parts are made on the premises. The store is something like a large shop complete with a counter, over which all the components issued are handed. Inside is a series of cubicles or partitions with shelves running almost to the roof. All the accessories are grouped and classified according to their kind and are identified by letters and numbers. Here, for example, are tiers of shelves—it would perhaps be truer to call them receptacles—containing electric components. Most of them are wrapped, and all are marked with an 'E' and a number. Here we find contacts, switches, wire, and the hundreds of items associated with the electrical side of the work. Farther on we see a number of boxes marked M 1, M 2, and so on. These contain motors, and there are *forty different kinds.*

In another section we find metal components of all descriptions subdivided into groups such as nails and screws, nuts and bolts, springs of all descriptions. The store-keeper can 'lay his finger' on any particular article required at a moment's notice, and the whole store bears evidence of his efficiency. Lastly, we are shown into another department where fabrics of many kinds are kept. Here are felts of varied texture, thickness, and colour, and skins of all descriptions. Most of the leather is sheepskin; but there is also a quantity of kid-skin, quite thin and soft to the touch. We are very pleased when the store-keeper insists on our handling a number of samples, for there is a joy in the feel of this beautiful, supple, white leather. He shows us 'split', very fine and soft in texture, and used for 'interior pneumatic work for primary movements'; 'pneumatic', very soft but slightly thicker and very strong; bedding', a heavier skin, still very soft and used for clamping joints; 'half-strained', a 'good' strong sheepskin leather which has been toughened and stretched by a special process; 'full-strained', and lastly 'brown pallet', which are the stoutest and strongest of all, being used for bellows work, cornering, and wherever the work is heaviest and the strain greatest. We cannot hope to see everything in this extensive store, but at least we can form some idea of the complexities attendant upon organ-building on a large scale.

Now we are taken into the mill; it is really two mills in one. In the first, the wood is prepared for the marking-out shop, which we will see next. After being marked for boring and cutting, the boards are sent to the fine mill where these operations are carried out. To save a return journey, let us visit both sections of this department before proceeding to the marking shop. The timber 'in the rough' is first cut to length on the circular saw and is then taken to the 'planers'.

The surface planer is a machine having a steel table about six feet in length and perhaps some three feet in width. Running across the centre of the table is a slit or channel through which, just barely protruding, is a revolving cutter (Fig. 91). It consists of a long roller having two projecting cutting-

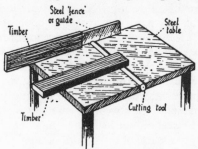

FIG. 91. *Planing machine.*

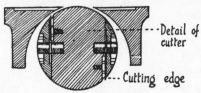

FIG. 92. *Detail of cutter.*

edges (section shown at Fig. 92). At one side of the table is a 'square fence' at right-angles to the surface of the table and also to the direction of the cutting-blades. These revolve at great speed and as the board is slowly pressed or pushed across the gap it is cut by the revolving blades. The board has now a perfectly true face-surface and this becomes the basis of all subsequent operations. The board is next placed on edge against the 'square fence' so that the cutter prepares the first edge at right-angles to the finished 'face'. The board is inverted and the second edge is similarly prepared.

It is now taken to a 'thicknessing' machine having (Fig. 93) a steel table similar to that which we have just seen, but in addition there is another table or plate of steel fixed above

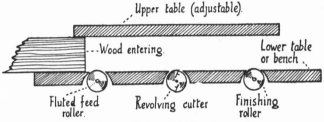

FIG. 93. *Sectional view of thicknessing machine.*

and parallel to it. The upper table can be raised or lowered to vary the distance between the two surfaces. These can be checked by means of a carefully marked brass gauge something like a vertical rule, affixed to the machine. The movable table can be raised or lowered with absolute precision by means of a handle, which the operator turns while watching the gauge. When the machine has been 'set' the board is 'fed' through the two surfaces or tables. It is received by a fluted feed-roller and this 'takes hold' of the board and forces it irresistibly towards the cutter, which pares off the superfluous wood. The board is driven towards another roller, quite smooth, and this compresses slightly, as it rolls out the issuing board, which by now is beautifully finished and absolutely true to measurement. This completes the preparation of the wood. The operators are working to specified measurements supplied to them by the organ designer. Let us suppose that the wood so prepared has been marked out and returned to the fine mill for further treatment. There are many machines here, the first we see

being a fret-saw. It has a large bow of lancewood and gut
(Fig. 94) fastened to the top of the machine. The saw-blade

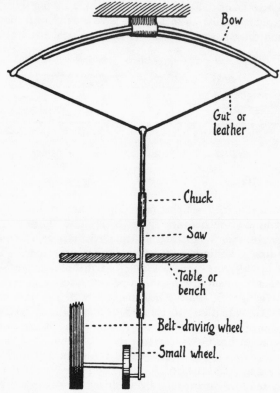

FIG. 94. *Bow-saw.*

passes through a narrow slot in the metal table. The small
wheel shown revolves very quickly, causing the saw to move
up and down while the blade is kept taut by the tension
of the bow. The machine is used for cutting all kinds

of shapes of the fret-work variety. Next we are shown a spindle moulding-machine, used for cutting mouldings of all kinds which might be needed for the case work. It consists simply of a steel bench having a hole in the middle of it, through which projects a spindle (see Fig. 95). This is

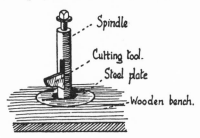

Spindle

Cutting tool.

Steel plate

Wooden bench.

FIG. 95. *Spindle moulding-machine.*

'split', having an aperture down the middle so that tools or 'cutters' may be inserted and securely fixed. The tool, whose cutting-edge is shaped according to the moulding required, projects like a tooth. The spindle can be made to revolve at high speed (3,500 revs. p.m.), and as the operator pushes the board against the revolving spindle the 'tooth' cuts the moulding as the wood passes by. All kinds of moulding can be made, different tools being inserted according to the pattern required.

Another interesting machine is used for mortising, which may be described briefly as the cutting of a hole or trench in one piece of wood to receive the end of another part. The machine, something like a stamping or drilling machine, operates a special composite tool consisting of a square, hollow chisel, having within it a drill. The tools, varying in size from one inch to a quarter of an inch, are placed in the machine. There are two wheels by which the operator can move the cutting-tool backwards, forwards, or sideways, and a lever which controls up-and-down movement. As the hollow chisel descends, the drill inside it revolves, paring away the wood within it. There are other machines we would like to examine, such as a saw-bench which can be adjusted for cross-cutting ends at any angle, and a sand-papering machine for finishing or cleaning up work, but there is much to be seen and we must pass on.

Adjoining the mill we are now leaving is the marking-out shop. The men at work here transfer the ideas of the organ designer from the plans supplied to the wood, which, when 'made up' to their measurements and markings, will form the main part of the finished instrument. They mark out such work as sound- and unit-boards, contact rails for selector-boards, and all similar parts; in fact, they prepare for the machinists and finishers everything to do with action, console, and pipe-sections. In the case of the pipes, however, we shall find that these are marked out by the pipe-makers themselves. At the moment, the markers are at work on a sound-board main action, which we shall understand when we get to the sound-board department (p. 141). The sound-board is really a misnomer, for makers often use the word when referring to the whole of that part which has to do with the 'speaking' of the pipes. To prevent confusion, we will use the word 'sound-board' when speaking of the table, the slides and bearers, and the upper board (see Fig. 104, p. 142). These together form the top of the wind-chest which contains or conserves the wind-pressure, conducted thither by a wind trunk.

The men are using special scaling rods, which are simply long rulers six or seven feet in length, having marks at intervals along them. The markers work from large-scale drawings or prints, and they must be very accurate in their marking.

When their work is completed it will be returned to the fine mill which we have just left. Here the machinists will bore, mortise, or shape the various parts of the structure, working to these markings and directions. The parts will then be

FIG. 96. MODERN ALL-ELECTRIC CONSOLE

DESCRIPTION: on extreme left and right—above—are the draw-knob jambs (i.e. panels) bearing the draw-knobs in six groups, namely: on left, *Swell, Pedal, Couplers* (also voltmeter) ; on right, *Solo, Great, Choir* (also blower-starter).

Behind these jambs are the motive solenoids, operating draw-knobs. The solenoids are controlled, in groups, by the appropriate thumb pistons—seen immediately under each manual (or keyboard).

Behind the music desk—top middle—which can be lifted, is the selector-board, which is described on page 130.

The names, in descending order, of the manuals are *Solo* (uppermost), *Swell, Great,* and *Choir.*

Below is the piston bank, bearing the toe pistons. In the centre are two balanced pedals, operating the louvres (see p. 129): left, *Solo pedal,* and right, *Swell pedal.* Under these are the pedal keys.

(By the courtesy of Wm. Hill & Son and Norman & Beard, Ltd.)

returned for approval before being dispatched to the respective departments which deal with them.

And now, after climbing a wooden staircase, we find ourselves in the console shop. We are introduced to the foreman, who takes us at once to the console—nearing completion —of a large church organ that is being modernized and electrified. (A modern console[1]—Fig. 96—is shown facing p. 129.) The old console will be removed and this one is to take its place. As it is a fine example, and one typical of its kind, we will study it in some detail under the expert guidance of the foreman, who is a master of his craft. It consists of a keyboard section of three manuals or rows of keys, which are played by the fingers, and a pedal-board below for the feet. At either side of the console are many draw-knobs controlling the various groups of pipes. When a draw-knob is moved to the 'on' position, the slide under the rank of pipes with which it corresponds will move automatically into the open position and the pipes will be ready to 'speak' when the keys are depressed and the pallets opened (see Figs. 104–108, pp. 142 and 143). Under each manual or keyboard we see a number of thumb pistons, and these, by a touch, can bring into action combinations of stops which 'belong' to the manual under which they are placed. We will see how they work in a moment. Immediately above the pedal-board is a series of toe-pistons. These control automatically various combinations of stops. In addition, there are foot-pedals here to operate swell-boxes for each main group of pipes. The 'swell' controls the volume of sound emitted by the pipes, which are enclosed in a chamber called the swell-box, one side of which consists of a line of shutters or louvres something like a venetian blind. These can be opened or closed by the action of the swell-pedal, thus increasing or diminishing the volume or intensity of the emerging sound.

Immediately in front of where the organist will be, and above the uppermost manual, there is what is called a selector-

---

[1] The console shown is not that described in the text, but is similar to it.

board. It consists of a large panel of ebonite and contains a great number of switches—actually there are two hundred and forty. There are five in each column, counting downwards, and forty-eight of these 'fives', counting horizontally. The switches are divided into four main groups, and here a little explanation is necessary. In a church or concert-hall organ each manual represents or controls a 'sub-organ', complete in itself, which can play quite independently and apart from the remainder of the instrument. The word 'organ' is used very generally to denote either the complete instrument or, to use the word we have just coined, any of the sub-organs, and each of these has its own special name, such as 'Swell' organ, 'Choir' organ, or 'Pedal' organ, and is known more familiarly as the 'Swell', 'Choir', 'Pedal', and 'Great' respectively.

The 'Swell' is the name usually given to the sub-organ associated with the uppermost manual. Next below this is the 'Great', and immediately under it is the 'Choir'. The 'Pedal', though having but thirty keys or pedals, can also, to a less extent, act independently.

To return to the selector-board, the first group of switches consists of fifteen rows of five. (Under each column of five is the name of the stop concerned.) This group belongs primarily to the Swell organ. We saw a moment ago at each side of the console a panel of draw-knobs. There is, by the way, some ambiguity about the nomenclature of stops, pistons, and draw-knobs. To prevent this we shall in future refer to the knobs, which can be pushed in or pulled out, as draw-knobs, and the word 'stop' when we are referring to the complete unit represented by the draw-knob, the action connected therewith, and the entire set of pipes which actually emits the sound. Thus the trumpet stop will mean the whole of that part of the organ actually concerned with the production of the trumpet tone.

Suppose now that the organist wishes to 'set' his stops on the Swell organ, which is controlled primarily from the swell or uppermost manual. He operates a switch for each stop he wishes to use, according to the combination of stops he has in mind. Let us try setting a 'selection' for ourselves. We choose any of the stops we wish to use, manipulate the particular switches controlling them, and then press the first of the thumb-pistons. Immediately, and to our surprise, all the draw-knobs of the stops we have chosen move out, towards us. We press the next piston and all the draw-knobs go in again. But we could have set another combination for the second thumb-piston, so that on being pressed it would have put out of action any stops controlled by the first piston, while retaining those required in the second combination and bringing into action any new stops to be introduced.

In each section of this selector-board similar combinations can be arranged for the other manuals, the net result being that the organist can set any combination of stops for any part or parts of the entire organ, and these can be brought in, or 'cut out', simply by the action of pressing the particular thumb or toe pistons concerned. The combinations possible are inexhaustible.

Let us now go behind the console and see how it works. The draw-knobs are actuated electrically by means of magnetic action. Each piston has an electrical contact which is connected with a switch on the front panel, and also with the thumb-piston or pistons which control it. Behind the console we are shown a control unit which might be termed the brain or nerve centre, known as the piston relay chest, a compartment that looks something like the inside of a wireless set. It contains a number of electro-magnetic units. Each one controls a stop, and when the switch on the selector-board has been put on, and the thumb-piston pressed, an electrical contact is established which energizes the control unit. This sends, as it were, a message to the draw-knob concerned. In other words, it completes the electrical circuit and so operates the magnet which causes the draw-knob to be extended, or withdrawn, as the case may be. We cannot help feeling a little bewildered at this, our first experience of electric control. It is so un-canny, so obviously efficient.

Now let us see something of the manufacture of the console itself. First the timber—Oregon pine in this instance—for the

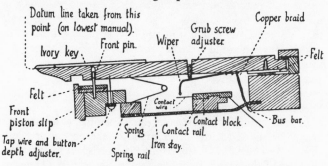

FIG. 97. *Sectional view of an organ key, showing electric contact.*

[*Note: this is a key on the u. .rmost keyboard—or manual; the key is inclined from the horizontal to facilitate playing.*]

main frame, after being 'fine-milled', is sent to the console room. Here the foreman 'checks it up' by the measurements with which he has been supplied. The parts are strongly bolted together, 'cleaned up', and sent down to the painting and polishing department to be 'finished off'. The frame comes back looking something like a bench.

Next the key-frames are fitted. These are usually made of oak and on each frame a keyboard will be mounted. The keyboards and keys are made by a firm which specializes in this work, and the processes are very similar to those we saw when studying pianoforte manufacture. The fitter-up takes out each key in order to fit the contact-rail (see Fig. 97). To this the contact-blocks are glued, one for each key on the keyboard, and each block contains the requisite number of contact wires. As many as nine wires may be mounted on

each contact-block, the number varying according to the
specification of the particular job being constructed (a contact-

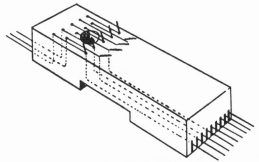

FIG. 98. *Contact block.*

block is shown at Fig. 98). A bus-bar is fixed to the back-
pin rail running the whole length occupied by the keys.

To the under-side of each key a contact-wiper is screwed
(see Fig. 99). It consists of a
strip of phosphor-bronze to
which a silver tab or length
of silver wire, and also a
short piece of copper wire
braid, are soldered. All the
wire braids are also fixed
to the bus-bar and convey
current to the nine contacts, in
the contact-block, where a
key is depressed. The grub-
screws which give the neces-

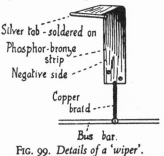

FIG. 99. *Details of a 'wiper'.*

sary adjustment to the contact-wiper are screwed into the
holes bored to receive them, one for each key. The keys are now
put back into the key-frame and the depth-adjusters fixed and
regulated. The springs which provide the resistance to the
fingers are now inserted. This resistance is called the 'touch'

and is generally three and a half ounces for each key. Modern cinema organs often have what is termed 'double touch', whereby the keys can be pressed half-way down to complete one set of electric contacts, and thus cause to sound certain pipes or combinations of pipes; but, in addition, the keys can be still farther depressed, making an entirely new set of contacts. These are added to the first, causing a different combination of stops to sound. The first touch in such a case is three and a half ounces, as before, while the second, which completely depresses the key, requires an additional pressure of three and a half ounces, making a total of seven ounces (each key).

When finally fixing the manuals in position, the fitter-up has to be very careful of what he calls the datum line. The tips of the keys (see Fig. 97, p. 132) on the lowest manual form the datum line, and all measurements are taken from it. Apparently certain standards of measurement are fixed by the Royal College of Organists and these are scrupulously observed by the maker. The pedal-board is now fixed in correct relationship with the datum line and the console begins to assume something approaching its finished appearance. The upper manuals, with their front slips (see Fig. 97) already prepared to receive the thumb-pistons, are 'fixed into position'. In smaller church organs three pistons for each manual is usual, while in the larger instruments five are provided on each piston slip. The pistons and the various appliances, such as swell pedals, which are worked by the feet, are similarly fixed.

Now the draw-knobs or stop-keys (see Fig. 96, facing p. 129) are inserted. In some organs draw-knobs are used, in others stop-keys are employed. Where stop-knobs, i.e. draw-knobs, are provided, they are fitted in 'stop-jambs' or panels. These are placed one at either end of the manuals and at an angle which will be most convenient for the organist. In the case of stop-keys, these are placed in a convenient 'sweep' over the upper manual and extending some distance on either side. In either case the panels or jambs are supplied by the case-work department all ready for mounting and receiving the stop-keys or knobs. When these have been assembled, the console is ready for the electrician, but before seeing him at work it is necessary to explain the action of a single key and find out just what happens when it is depressed. As the key descends (Fig. 97, p. 132) the 'wiper' is forced against the silver wires of its corresponding contact-block, which is mounted on the contact-rail. An electric circuit is thus completed; the current passes from the bus-bar via the link braid to the wiper, and thence through the fine wires of the contact-block to others on the under-side of the contact-rail, each wire being fixed in such a way as to form a kind of terminal to which another wire is soldered or otherwise secured. (The complete wiring and circuits are shown at Fig. 115, p. 156.) For every single contact, on each note, a separate wire is provided, and, to take the very simplest case possible, i.e. where only one contact is used for each key, a wire is led from the farthest key—say at the left extremity of the keyboard, and as it proceeds along the under-side of the contact-rail it is joined by a wire from the next adjacent key, and the next, and so on, until by the time the initial wire has reached the opposite end of the keyboard to that from which it started, it has been joined by sixty others, and ends as a cable containing sixty-one wires or leads, i.e. one for each note of the keyboard. But it is very rare to find only one contact in use for each key, and as many as nine separate silver wires, each representing a circuit, may be found in each contact-block, and for every individual contact in use a separate wire must be taken. Thus it can be imagined that for one key-board—or manual—alone there may be hundreds of separate wires in the cable conveying the current to its next destination. When we consider, further, that there may be four or five separate manuals, each with its hundreds of contacts and currents to be conveyed, we begin to get some idea of the complexity of a modern organ. Now let us follow the cable we have just seen, to find out what happens to it. It leads to

135

the test-board, which serves several useful purposes. Firstly, it obviates the congestion that might be caused through end-less cables multiplying and being lost sight of; in other words, it acts as a kind of sorting office, or clearing station, where all the wires are separated, identified, and 'fixed' for further use.

Secondly, it enables the builder to test all his wiring in the console itself when searching for faulty connexions. At the same time it should be observed that the test-board just mentioned is not an essential, but is rather in the nature of a convenience. From an all-electric console in what might be termed a 'straightforward church organ job', the main cable might well be taken straight to the sound-board section, where its component wires would be connected to their appropriate terminals.

In some organs, and more particularly in those built for cinemas, the wiring is rendered infinitely more complicated by the employment of what is known as 'extension', which, strictly speaking, should be explained when we come to the study of pipes. For the moment it will suffice to say that pipes vary greatly in size and consequently in pitch. Each set or rank of pipes is identified, for purposes of pitch, by the length of the lowest and longest pipe it contains. Thus, the very deep pipes are known as thirty-two foot, or simply as 'thirty-two', pipes because the longest pipe in the rank measures approximately thirty-two feet in length. Next are the 'six-teens'—an octave higher in pitch—and the 'eights'—an octave higher still. The eight-foot ranks give what might be termed ordinary pianoforte pitch. Above this are the four- and two-foot stops, the former an octave and the latter two octaves above the 'eights', or above pianoforte pitch.

Organ-builders used to add, for each additional stop on the organ, a complete set of pipes, even where these were only an octave above or below the existing stops. Astute organ-builders, however, upon the advice of organists, began to simplify such additions by extending the existing rank by an octave, or two octaves, upward or downward. To take a simple instance: where a sixteen- and a four-foot stop are to be added to an existing eight-foot rank, the builder, using 'extension', simply adds a complete octave of pipes to each 'end' and thereby provides three complete stops of sixteen-, eight-, and four-foot stops, respectively: and all are of homogeneous quality. He thus saves extra material, labour, and expense, while the organist can add a four or a sixteen stop without doubling or trebling the notes which would have been common to all three ranks if a complete rank had been added for each additional stop.

To return to the question of wiring which we were considering (on p. 136): although extension results in a considerable saving where additional pipes are concerned, it also involves the incorporation of a much more complicated wiring installation, so much so that in the case of cinema organs, where the extension system is employed, one might say *ad nauseam*, the wiring becomes so complex that additional frames, or panels, have to be provided to deal with it. These components are so complicated that it would be futile within the limits of this study to elucidate their manifold complexities.

The foreman, who has been explaining the console, advises us to 'have another look' at the piston relay chest and also at the electrically operated draw-knobs which they control. He tells us that in many organs the draw-knobs themselves are moved by electro-pneumatic action, while in others this may be accomplished by electro-magnetic action alone. In this case the console, being entirely electric, does not use any other motive power—i.e. it does not employ pneumatic action at all.

The switches on the selector-board which we recently saw, the control units in the relay chest, the test-board terminals, the draw-knob mechanism, and the thumb, and toe, pistons are all connected electrically. When any particular switch on the selector-board is put 'on', and the piston controlling it is also brought into operation, the magnetic units in the relay chest send the current which energizes the magnets operating the draw-knobs, and these are seen to move outwards when the finger- or toe-pistons are pressed in. When another piston is operated the contacts are broken and the draw-knobs return to their normal 'off' position while other circuits are completed, according to the combination set at the selector-board, and the corresponding draw-knobs move outwards to the 'on' position. Before leaving the test-board we notice at the base a separate line of terminals belonging to the return wires from the draw-knobs. It consists of two separate rows of 'points', each being marked with the names of the stops corresponding to those on the console.

We saw a little while ago (p. 135) how the wires from the keyboard were put together to become a cable, which itself was joined up with others to form a multiple cable. Since we cannot possibly follow all the wires to their respective destinations, we will content ourselves by seeing what happens to the cable leading from the keyboard. It takes us to the 'switch-stack', which might be described as a 'half-way house' between the console and pipe—including the action—section. Before describing it in detail we will find out what it actually does. It really joins up the circuits, when coupling (which was explained on p. 117) is employed. We are fortunate in being allowed to study for a moment the designer's drawing relating to the work in hand. The chart shows an organ containing Swell, Great, and Choir manuals, and below them the Pedals. With the aid of the chart from which we have taken a sketch (Fig. 100, p. 139), let us consider three simple cases which might arise when the organ is being played.

In the first, let us suppose the organist has put on a number of stops at the Swell manual and wishes to play these from the Swell keyboard. We find the wires simply passing through the switch-stack in the Swell bus-bar to the action and pipes.

In the second case, suppose the organist wishes to play a stop on the Swell organ from the Great manual, he puts on the

Swell-to-Great draw-knob, thereby putting switch 1 into contact with the Swell bus-bar, which means that the electric circuit from the Great manual, via the bus-bar to the Swell organ,

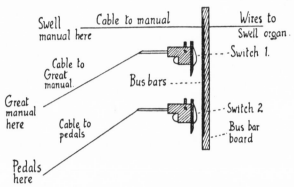

FIG. 100. *Circuits, wiring, &c., illustrating part of the coupling arrangements (see also Fig. 103).*

is now complete except for the pressing of the Great keys, which, when they make contact, cause the pipes to sound.

In the third case, the organist, wishing to play the lower notes of the Swell from the pedals, puts on the Swell-to-Pedal stop. This causes switch 2 to operate, making contact which passes from the Swell via the switch-stack to the pedal, which, when depressed, completes the circuit and causes the pipes to 'speak'. To avoid too much complication we have omitted to mention that in each of the above cases the circuit is continued between the switch-stack and the action—and pipes.

The cases above mentioned are but examples of many which might occur, but the principle is the same. Now let us examine the switch-stack, which is much too complicated to describe in detail. To avoid complexity let us look at a single unit of bus-bars and switch (Figs. 101 and 102, p. 140). The bus-bars, sixty-one in number—i.e. one for each key on the manual—consist of narrow strips of phosphor-bronze, about one-eighth of an inch in width and not much thicker than three or four leaves of this book. Their length depends upon

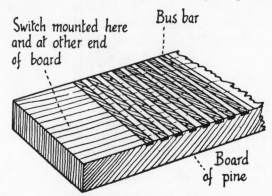

FIG. 101. *Part of a bus-bar unit.*

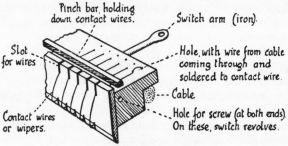

FIG. 102. *Part of a switch.*

the number of switches employed. These are mounted close together as shown (Fig. 101), on a board of pine in which grooves have been prepared to receive them. They are kept in position by short brass nails at intervals along the strips.

The cable from the keyboard is 'broken down' at the switch-stack and each wire is soldered to its corresponding bus-bar. When the switch comes into operation it makes contact with all the bus-bars (see Fig. 103). The switch is a very ingenious appliance. The 'switch' arm (see Fig. 102, p. 140) is operated

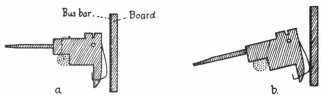

Fig. 103. a. *Switch—off*; b. *Switch making contact.*

by electro-pneumatic action and the drawing gives a good idea of its construction. It revolves on screws, one at either end. The wiping action of the contact-wires is worth a special note. Each wire actually wipes or rubs the bus-bar adjacent to it, thus ensuring a clean contact. This reminds us that in the key-contact which we saw the wires were of silver. On asking why silver is used, we are told another interesting fact, namely, that silver oxide is a good conductor of electricity. On the switch there are sixty-one wires corresponding to and opposite the sixty-one bus-bars. In the drawing (Fig. 102, p. 140) the cable can be seen. The wires pass through the holes in the switch and are soldered to the terminals of the contact-wires.

Practically all the constituents we have seen are made on the premises of this firm, but we must omit many of the smaller details of manufacture, partly because they resemble work we have seen here and elsewhere, but also because of the time it would take to see everything.

And so we proceed to the sound-board department. As we have seen, the word 'sound-board' is really a misnomer, for it is often used to denote the wind-chest (Fig. 104, p. 142, and at Figs. 105–8, p. 143) and includes the upper board, table, and grid. At first sight the whole structure looks extremely complicated, but we will 'take it to pieces' and examine each part separately, so that we may be able to understand just what

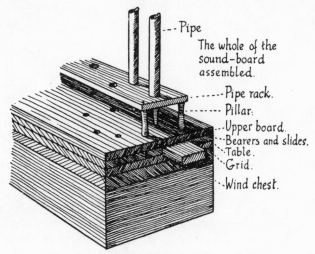

--- Pipe

The whole of the sound-board assembled.

------ Pipe rack.

------ Pillar.

--- Upper board.

··· Bearers and slides.
··· Table.
··· Grid.

··· Wind chest.

FIG. 104. *Sound-board and wind-chest assembled.*

happens when an organist puts on a particular stop and plays a series of notes.

At Fig. 104 the whole assembly is shown, while at Fig. 108 (p. 143) we see the wind-chest, or 'well'. This contains the 'wind', or air under pressure, which is conducted thither by a wind-trunk (not shown). This is simply a large pipe of wood or metal. Over the wind-chest is placed the grid (Fig. 107), and above this again is the table (Fig. 106) with its slides and bearers. Over the table lies the upper board, to which are attached the pillars supporting the pipe rack (shown in Fig. 104), the latter holding the pipes in position. (All these

142

parts are shown in the diagrams, which should be carefully studied before proceeding further.)

To continue: under the channels or air-spaces in the grid are

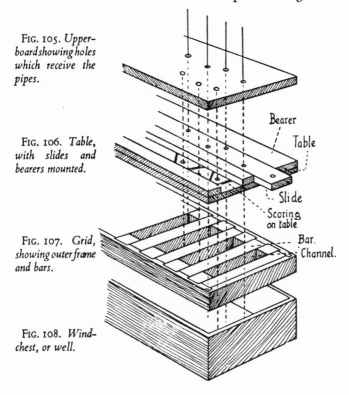

FIG. 105. *Upper-board showing holes which receive the pipes.*

FIG. 106. *Table, with slides and bearers mounted.*

Bearer

Table

Slide

Scoring on table

FIG. 107. *Grid, showing outer frame and bars.*

Bar.

Channel.

FIG. 108. *Wind-chest, or well.*

pallets, one for each aperture (Fig. 109, p. 144). These are operated by electro-pneumatic action from the key-contacts, which, when depressed, open the pallets, giving the air in the wind-chest access to the underside of the table lying im-mediately above the grid. Here the wind must stay, unless the slides are in such a position that the holes which have been bored through them lie exactly over the corresponding holes in the table. In the diagram there is provision for two slides, i.e. two stops; for each slide represents a complete stop or

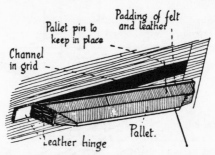

Padding of felt and leather

Pallet pin to keep in place

Channel in grid

Leather hinge

Pallet.

FIG. 109. *Pallet—open—on under-side of grid.*

range of pipes. Usually one finds more than two stops on a sound-board, but for our purpose two will suffice. The slides are controlled from the console by means of draw-knobs, or stop-keys, each being connected with the slide to which it belongs. When the organist 'puts on' a stop he is really bringing into operation a slide which is so adjusted that it can move backward or forward. In the 'off' position the holes in the slide lie over the 'bars' of the grid, while the holes in the table are covered by the solid part of the slide. In the 'on' position, however, each hole in the slide lies exactly over the corresponding hole beneath it, so that wherever a pallet is open the wind has access from the wind-chest via the air-vents in the grid, and thence, by way of the table and slide, through the holes in the upper board, to the pipes, which are thus made to 'speak' or sound. . . .

Let us just go over this again to summarize what happens. The organist puts 'on' a number of stops. The slides concerned move into the 'on' position. He depresses a number of keys and the pallets they control are opened. (We shall see how this happens later when we come to the action department.) Air under pressure from the wind-generator proceeds via the wind-trunk into the well and thence through the open pallets to the stops. Where the stops are 'closed' the wind remains: where they are open it proceeds through the table and upper board into the pipes, which then sound their respective notes. Perhaps on a future visit we may see all these parts being made; at the moment, although there are several sound-boards in evidence, there is no definite 'making' in process. . . .

We are fortunate this time, for a 'job' is actually being constructed, but we are told that we must 'begin at the beginning', and so we go with the foreman to his special table. He has a large, wide bench on which is the specification for the particular sound-board to be made. Three stops are to be provided and measurements are given restricting the size of the job to certain limits which are fixed by the designer of the instrument, or they may have been imposed by the technical expert who has to 'see the whole thing through'. There is also on the bench a very large plan mounted on cardboard. He is going to show us how he lays out his pipes on the table (i.e. the table of the sound-board) which he is about to make.

He shows us a curious collection of patterns arranged in sets and consisting of a number of metal disks, each having a small hole through the centre whereby they can be strung on a file, like so many bills or receipts. In some sets the patterns are square, while in others they are round, the former representing wood and the latter metal pipes. Each set is graded in size, with the smallest uppermost. Usually there are sixty-one disks on each file, one for each pipe or for each note on the keyboard. It is somewhat difficult to express just what they represent, but actually they are 'solid plans' of the pipes. When laid out on the 'specification' or on the board, which will become the table of the sound-board, they show the maker just how much room, or space, each pipe will occupy. Sometimes he finds that they overlap and then he must 'spread them out'—to use his own phrase. It is important that each pipe has ample room in which to 'speak'. Now we shall see how all these parts are made. First let us watch the construction of a grid. It consists of an outer frame with 'traverse' bars grooved and screwed into it (Fig. 107, p. 143). Wood 'fillings' are fitted and glued between the bars to determine the length of the openings left for the pallets. The sketch gives some idea of the finished grid, but in a large sound-board the grid is usually much wider than that shown, and the bars and channels extending beyond that part which is occupied by the pallets are 'sealed', or made air-tight, by having a strip of American cloth extending the whole length of the sound-board, and of sufficient width to cover all but the pallet section.

It must not be forgotten that all the work we have just seen has been carried out according to the instructions and markings set out by the foreman, who, in turn, is working to the stipulations supplied by the designer and his assistants in the drawing office. We have already seen something of this preparation, which, in the trade, is termed 'planting' a sound-board. The grid is really the foundation of the sound-board, for the spacing and extent of the air-grooves or channels really determines the limits within which the rest of the work must be confined. When the grid is completed the usual procedure is to prepare the table, slides, bearers, and upper-board, and fix them for boring before turning the work over for fixing the pallets. But we will see these processes on another occasion, when they are actually being carried out.

When the grid has been completed and 'finished off', the pallets are mounted. These are affixed on the under-side of the grid, which is turned over while this is being done. The pallets themselves are made of wood and their shape can be seen (Fig. 109, p. 144). They are bevelled to lessen the weight and also to minimize the surface-area exposed to air-pressure, for these pallets will lie within the wind-chest, which is fed from the wind-generator. Each pallet is fixed to the grid by means of a leather hinge. On the face-side is glued a layer of thick felt, and covering this is a layer of soft leather. The felt 'softens the blow' when the pallet closes and thus prevents noise, while the leather helps to ensure that no air will escape through the pallet to the table. The pallet is operated by means of a wire attached to the action (see Fig. 112, p. 153, and Fig. 113, p. 154). All the pallets are made and mounted, and the grid is complete.

The table (Fig. 106, p. 143) is next made. It consists of a solid slab of mahogany five-eighths of an inch thick. The slides, also of mahogany, and the bearers, probably of pine or some other reliable wood, are laid on the table and the upper board is placed over them. In short, the table, slides, bearers, and upper-board are assembled for boring. It is obvious that if the holes which are shown in the various sketches (Figs. 105–108, p. 143) are to 'agree', the best way of ensuring 'perpendicular alinement'—to coin a phrase—is to fasten all the parts close together before the boring is carried out.

When this process has been completed the various pieces are taken apart and the table is glued to the grid. The bearers and slides are nailed to the table. Half-inch panel nails are used and these are 'punched in'. The surface is then planed by hand to one 'dead level', i.e. bearers and slides form one level surface. The slides are now taken up again and all panel nails are removed. The bearers, of course, are allowed to remain fixed as they were. The bearers are next papered, that is, they are covered with white paper which is pasted to them. This is done to give clearance to the slides when the upper board is fixed over the table.

While this is being done the pipes are being fitted elsewhere into the rack-board and the upper board. And here we may explain the question of 'scoring'. Suppose a four- or five-stop sound-board to be part of a finished instrument, and that only one stop is being used. When the organist plays a chord it is obvious that the wind will have access to the under-side of the other slides, not in use. The wind-pressure—which is considerable—through the pallet holes, will tend to lift the slides by reason of the clearance allowed by the paper thickness which has been described. The organ-builder's problem is to find an outlet for this unwanted wind, other than to let it 'creep' round the slide and find its way to the pipes, which would begin to 'whimper' or make a whining noise. This he does by means of a system of 'scoring', whereby a number of separate channels or grooves are cut with a grooving tool, somewhat like a plane, in the table (these are shown in Fig. 106, p. 143) in such a way as to isolate each hole from its neighbour. The under-side of the upper board is similarly treated. The air pressure, instead of finding its way through into the pipes, is thus diverted or side-tracked towards the edges of the table and upper-board, and allowed to escape or 'trickle' away.

A short while ago we mentioned the fact that the larger pipes had to be 'spread' sometimes, in order to fit them or accommodate them in such a way that each pipe had 'speaking room'. If the pipes are placed too close to one another there is liable to be not only congestion, but also sound, or acoustic interference, between adjacent 'speaking' pipes, which would greatly impair the tone. The spreading of the pipes when necessary is done as follows. It is a general rule that the position of the slide holes must never be altered, for if this were done all kinds of complications would result. Only the upper board, as a rule, is concerned. In the diagrams (Fig. 105-108) it will be seen that the holes in the sound-board are drilled straight through, in line with those in the table and slides. Now let us look at the sketch (Fig. 110, p. 149), which shows (a) sectional view and (b) the corresponding markings on the upper side of the board, which were put there by the foreman. The numbers 1, 2, and 3 show where the holes lie on the table beneath, while at 1 (a), 1 (b), and 1 (c) are shown the

positions of the pipes themselves; or perhaps it would be clearer
if we said that they show where the holes will be bored so **as**

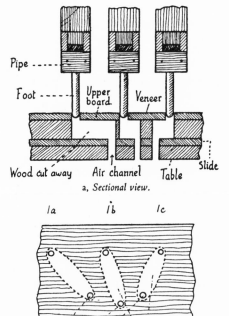

a, *Sectional view.*

b, *Plan of part of top surface of upper board.*

FIG. 110. *Showing how pipes are spread.*

to receive the pipes after being 'spread'. The holes at 1 (*a*),
1 (*b*), and 1 (*c*) are made and the board turned over. Channels
or grooves are then cut to convey the air from the holes in the
table and slides to the new pipe holes.

There is still a lot to be done before the work is completed, and we must return to the grid for a moment. After the pallets are correctly fixed in position and each hinge, of sheep-skin, glued to the under-side of the grid, a pallet-wire is fixed to each pallet (see Fig. 91, p. 124) and also to a spring-rail which runs the length of the grid. Each spring is attached to its appropriate pallet. A motor, which will be explained in a moment, is prepared for each pallet. The motors are fixed to the bottom board, in a line and in such a position that, when assembled and connected up, each motor will lie directly under the pallet which it will operate. The whole sound-board is now put together piece by piece. Three sides which have been prepared are assembled, and the grid, the table, containing the slides, and the upper board, with the pillars and pipe-racks already in position to receive the pipes, are screwed down into position. The bottom board is 'bedded' with leather and screwed on. The fourth side is the last to be added. This is known as the 'front' or 'inspection board', and is screwed on in such a way that it can be readily removed to give access to the wind-chest for repairs or adjustments. Before this is finally fixed, however, any connexions which still remain to be made are completed and the whole of the mechanism is given a final testing. Provision has been made for connecting the wind-trunk with the 'well', and the sound-board as such is now complete, but it still lacks a very important and com-plementary unit, namely, the 'action'; and here we must sus-pend our observations for a while, and before our next visit is due we will find out a little about the purpose and functions of actions in general.

The best approach to the question will be to consider the working of the older and purely mechanical organ (see Fig. 89, p. 117). The key was connected by a 'sticker' to a 'square', which in turn operated a 'tracker'. This was attached to a second 'square', which pulled down a wire connected to the pallet. All these processes are really part of the action. When we consider that the whole of this operation, from keyboard to pallet, was dependent upon the pressure of the organist's fingers, we can see that his work was by no means easy, and in some cases it was only by considerable physical force that he could depress the keys at all, especially when large numbers of stops were in action; each stop added would tend to increase the resistance to his fingers.

To minimize this difficulty several enterprising builders began to experiment with pneumatic action. The underlying principle of this was that bellows inflated from the air pressure in the wind-chest could become an agent to move levers, pallets, and the like. When deflated they could be made to collapse by the pressure of the wind, outside them, but within the wind-chest. The two processes, i.e. inflation and deflation, were made possible by an ingenious arrangement of valves (Fig. 112, p. 153). At first, this was used only between the keyboard and the first square, which it replaced (Fig. 90, p. 118). Later the principle was applied to the control of the pallets themselves, thus rendering the second tracker and square unnecessary. At first only single motors were employed, but later, primary motors were used to inflate or deflate secondary larger and more powerful motors, and even tertiary motors were in turn added. A curious thing was that the addition of these motors did not appreciably delay the action; they are practically instantaneous. Motors are really bellows, made of wood and sheepskin (see Fig. 111, p. 152, where types of motors are shown). They are inflated from the existing wind supply contained in the various action-chests. Sometimes, as in the case of smaller primary motors, they are used simply to operate valves to which they are attached, or they may be more definitely employed as 'motors', i.e. 'movers', as when opening pallets (see Fig. 112, p. 153) or operating slides (see Fig. 116, p. 157). In some organs the whole action is pneumatic, being operated by wind alone. In more modern organs, however, the tendency is to employ electro-magnetic action to replace the primary valves (see Fig. 115, p. 156). The manufacture of these motors hardly merits a detailed description, since their construction is quite simple, and we will concern ourselves more with the way in which they function. Let us

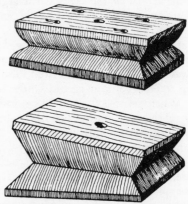

FIG. 111. *Types of motors in general use. Above, oblong type—trade name, 'square drop': very powerful. Below, hinged type, acting directly as a lever.*

look at Fig. 90 (p. 118) for a moment and try to understand how a simple motor of the earliest type was operated. The key has been depressed and the sticker has raised the lever and also allowed the exhaust valve to close. Wind from the key-chest has filled the motor, causing it to open, thus acting as a pneumatic lever which operates the first square and consequently the second, to which it is attached, thus opening the pallet. The resistance of the air pressing on the pallet, and also of the pallet spring, is overcome by the motive power of the motor, which is made of sufficient size to ensure this.

In all cases, we have to remember that for each key and pallet there will be a separate and complete motive unit. Now consider Fig. 112, p. 153, and Fig. 113, p. 154. Here is a more complicated application of the use of motors. There are three

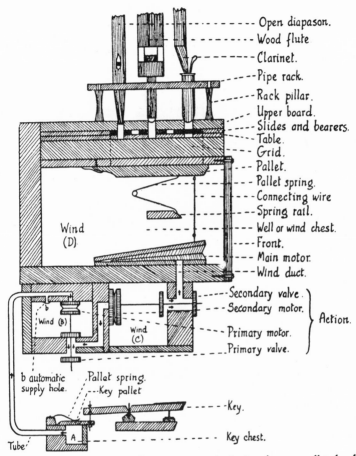

Open diapason.

Wood flute

Clarinet.

Pipe rack.

Rack pillar.

Upper board.

Slides and bearers.

Table.

Grid.

Pallet.

Pallet spring.

Connecting wire

Spring rail.

Well or wind chest.

Front.

Main motor.

Wind duct.

Wind
(D)

Secondary valve.

Secondary motor.

Action.

Wind (B)

Wind
(C)

Primary motor.

Primary valve.

b automatic
supply hole.

Pallet spring.

Key pallet

Key.

Key chest.

Tube

A

FIG. 112. *Sectional diagram showing* Pneumatic Action, *key up, pallet closed.*

Position in pressure- or wind-chambers:

In A (key chest), Key pallet closed: pressure on; in B, Primary motor inflated: valve closed to pressure, but open to exhaust; in C, Motor exhausted through primary valve: valve closed to exhaust, but open to pressure; in D (well), Main motor inflated: pallet closed.

153

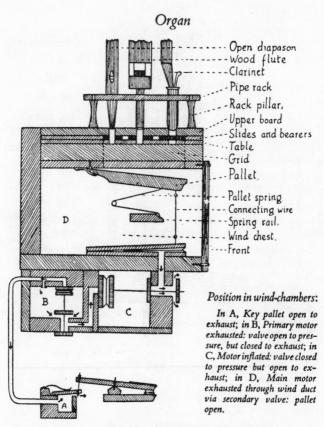

Open diapason
Wood flute
Clarinet
Pipe rack
Rack pillar,
Upper board
Slides and bearers
Table
Grid
Pallet.
Pallet spring
Connecting wire
Spring rail.
Wind chest.
Front

Position in wind-chambers:

In A, Key pallet open to exhaust; in B, Primary motor exhausted: valve open to pressure, but closed to exhaust; in C, Motor inflated: valve closed to pressure but open to exhaust; in D, Main motor exhausted through wind duct via secondary valve: pallet open.

FIG. 113. *Pneumatic action: key down, pallet open.*

motors in use, namely, the primary, secondary, and tertiary or main motors. In each chamber wind can proceed in either direction. In Fig. 112 the key is 'up'; the small pallet closes chamber A, which is filled with wind admitted through a small hole known as the automatic supply hole (b). This is a small boring ($\frac{3}{16}$ in. diameter) leading from chamber B to the wind–

tube. Over the hole a perforated paper is glued, and this allows wind to 'filter' through into the tube and thence to the key-chest (A). Thus, when the pallet is closed the pressure in 'A' and in the tube is sufficient to inflate the motor at 'B' and so

close chamber 'B' by means of the small valve which it operates, but at the same time opening a way to atmosphere whereby the secondary motor, in C, collapses under the wind pressure within chamber C. In doing so the secondary valve closes this chamber C to atmosphere and wind passes into the main motor, inflating it and holding the pallet in its closed position. When the key is depressed (see Fig. 113, p. 154) and the key pallet lifted, the wind is allowed to escape from the primary motor faster than the automatic supply hole admits it; the motor therefore collapses and the position of the secondary and tertiary motors is reversed and the pallet opens.

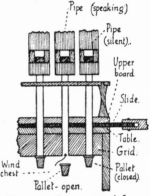

FIG. 114. *Cross section (of upper part of* Figs. 112 *and* 113) *showing slide—'on'—and pallets. Middle pipe is 'speaking'.*

At Fig. 115 (p. 156) the key makes an electrical contact when depressed and the armature operates the first valve, causing the primary motor to collapse. This closes the first valve to atmosphere and opens the second, so that the pressure within the wind-chest overcomes the large motor, causing it to collapse and thereby pulling down and opening the pallet to which it is attached.

There are innumerable variations of these systems in organ building, each maker having his own ideas and improvements, but in the main the principles are the same as those just described. One of the most ingenious and efficient applications

155

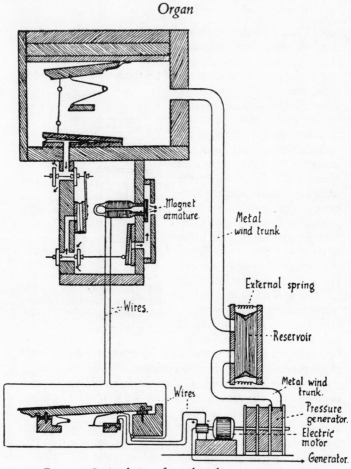

FIG. 115. *Sectional view of a modern electro-pneumatic organ.*

of the motor principle is shown (Fig. 116, p. 157). Here we
see a unit, of which there will be one for each slide mounted
in a rank at the end of the wind-chest, which moves the slide

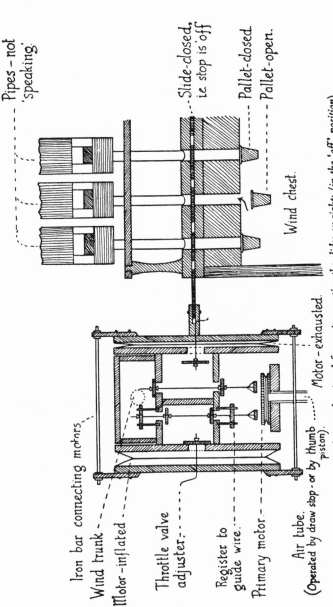

Pipes – not 'speaking'.

Slide–closed, i.e. stop is 'off'.

Pallet–closed.
Pallet–open.

Wind chest.

Iron bar connecting motors.
Wind trunk.
Motor–inflated.

Throttle valve adjuster.

Register to guide wire.

Primary motor.

Motor – exhausted.

Air tube.
(Operated by draw stop· or by thumb piston).

FIG. 116. *Sectional view, showing, left, a unit operating the slide; on right· (in the 'off' position).*

backwards and forwards. The primary motor, which is here seen at rest will, when inflated, raise both the 'buttons', which can be seen just above it. When the stop is 'off' the position is as shown. The valves work in opposite ways: in other words, the right-hand chamber is open to exhaust and closed to pressure, whereas that on the left is open to pressure and closed to atmosphere, so that the bellows is inflated as shown. When the draw-knob is put on, the wind enters the primary motor, which it inflates, thus reversing the position of both valves. The right-hand bellows is now inflated, while the other collapses, the arm moves to the right—in this case—and the slide moves with it so that the holes in both upper-board and slide are 'in line' and the pipes ready to 'speak' as their respective pallets are opened. The middle pipe would thus be actually sounding.

It is almost impossible to describe in detail how action-boards are made. From the various units we have been studying we must do our best to imagine a line or row of primary valves—sixty-one for each manual—and these are glued to a board which has been drilled ready to receive the valves and also for the various air channels as shown in the diagrams. Another complete set of secondary motors and valves will be assembled and glued or screwed to this, and when the whole 'action' is complete it will be thoroughly tested. Such a test is now being carried out in the sound-board department. Apparently the action has been affixed to the wind-chest, for the men who are working on it tell us that they are testing a 'sound-board', which is resting on two strong wooden trestles. It is electro-pneumatic, and accommodates six stops, representing six ranks each of sixty-one notes—or pipes.

Near the 'job' is a wind reservoir very much like that shown (at Fig. 117, p. 159). The wind pressure is regulated by placing iron bars whose weights are known across the top of the bellows section. The reservoir is kept charged by a flexible wind-trunk which evidently leads from a generator, but this we cannot see. Another trunk is connected to the sound-board.

There are two operators at work; one is lying under the sound-board and has two wires which are let down from above. He holds a 'live' negative wire to the bus-bar, which has soldered to it a lead from each magnet. He holds the live

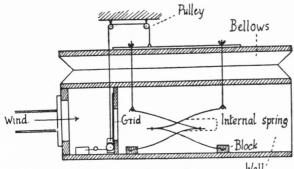

FIG. 117. *Sectional view of reservoir.*

positive wire to each positive terminal of a magnet, thus making contact, with the result that the magnet is energized and attracts the armature, which is the primary valve of the electro-pneumatic action (see Fig. 115, p. 156). From this point onwards the action is pneumatic, operating the valves and causing the pipes to 'speak', as already described.

The sound-board is so placed that the pipe-holes are uppermost. As the man underneath makes his contacts, the other tests the air-pressure emerging from the particular pipe-hole being examined. Sometimes he is satisfied by holding his hand a little way from, and over, the hole, sometimes he places a pipe into the hole and, by the way it 'speaks', can tell whether the action is working satisfactorily. Should the pressure be inadequate, the note in question must be checked at all stages—magnet, valves, motors, &c.—until the fault is detected and rectified.

Sometimes a pipe will sound when it should not do so, this

being due to the fact that air is reaching the pipe through some
fault in the structure. This is known as a 'cypher' and is one
of the organ-builder's bugbears. In modern organs there is
usually a contrivance inserted, called a ventil, and this can automatically cut off the wind supply to the whole rank, which
will remain silent until the fault can be located and rectified.

The completion of the action and sound-board leads us to
the pipes, but since we cannot have sound without *wind*, we
must now 'go back to the beginning' again, and find out what
we can about the motive power which animates the vast array
of silent pipes.

For hundreds of years this wind-pressure was supplied by
bellows of wood and leather, which were driven at first by
men called organ-blowers and later by engines of various kinds.

To-day, however, the majority of organ-builders use fans
for this purpose. Smaller organs are usually provided with a
single fan, which is so constructed that when it revolves it sucks
air through an aperture and passes it on at increased pressure
to the reservoirs (see Fig. 115, p. 156). In larger organs,
multiple pressure generators are installed. Three, four, or five
fans are placed in series, the first raising the pressure to perhaps two inches, the second to four, the third to six, and so on.

It should be explained here that when the builder speaks of
the pressure as being, say, two inches, he means two inches
above normal atmospheric pressure, and each inch equals five
pounds per square foot increase—or ·036 lb. to the square
inch. The pressure is measured by means of a wind-gauge
(or anemometer), which consists of a glass ⊔ tube with one
arm turned down thus ⌐⊔ and connected by a flexible
tube to a 'foot' which will fit into the pipe holes. The tube is
mounted on a board having a scale on it. The ⊔ section is
about half-full of water and normally the columns in each

arm are level and the instrument is 'at zero'. When the air is forced along the flexible pipe into the ⊔ tube the level in the first arm drops, while in the corresponding arm it rises, by exactly the same amount. An inch drop in the first column and a rise in the second of the same distance would actually mean a two-inch increase in the pressure being recorded.

To return to the fan: this is made entirely of metal and consists of an outer casing, which contains a circular fan having vanes or blades attached to it. These are shaped and fixed in such a way that when the fan revolves at high speed the vanes suck in the air through an aperture at one side of the machine into the chamber enclosed by the outer casing. At the other side is a circular outlet, some ten inches in diameter, to which a leather collar is fastened: this will be connected up with the main trunk of the organ.

If the wind generator be of the multiple type, several fans will be mounted on one long steel spindle, each in its own casing, all being connected in such a way that the air can proceed through one fan to the next. If different wind pressures are required, they may be taken direct from the fan concerned; thus a four-inch pressure trunk will be connected to the second fan, and a six-inch trunk to the third.

The manufacture of a wind generator is not of particular interest, the machines being constructed mostly of sheet iron reinforced at the joints with angle-bar iron (∟ section). One machine used in the construction of 'blowers' is rather interesting. The bars are supplied in straight lengths, and when a 'hoop' is required a bar is fed into a bending machine which contains several steel rollers and is worked by a handle with a long shaft. As the mechanic turns the handle, the rollers draw the bar in between them, and it emerges bent in such a way as to form a complete circle of the size required for the casing.

Organ

To this the sides of the case, cut to size and bent to shape, are riveted.

The revolving unit consists of a flat disk, and on one side the vanes, cut ready to shape, are riveted. On the other, circular flanges are fixed to prevent the wheel from 'edging' along, under the pressure of the air, and so wearing the bearing down on one side of the fan. When two fans are required they are generally put 'back to back', the air being drawn in at both sides, thus obviating the tendency to 'edge' along, which we have just mentioned. A shaped disk is riveted to the vanes and is of interest, for it resembles somewhat the bell of a brass wind instrument (⌒‿⌒) and it is spun on a large wooden matrix, at the lathe, in exactly the same way as we saw when visiting the bell-maker (see p. 75 and Fig. 55). In this case, however, the moulding implement is longer and more powerful, for the process requires more pressure.

The supports or legs upon which the fan stands are either cast or forged. The bearings carrying the spindle are made of gun-metal, which is much harder than brass, and are turned on the lathe. They are fixed over an oil-bath, and ring lubrication is employed. A brass ring of slightly larger diameter than the spindle is slipped over it to rest in a circular groove. As the spindle bearing the fans revolves, the ring, which has its lower portion immersed in oil, keeps turning round, bringing with it a sufficient quantity of oil to keep the axle and bearing lubricated. It is a useful and economical device.

The wind generator, when completely assembled, is provided with a driving-wheel which will be attached to an electric motor. Where necessary this, in turn, will be connected with a generator to provide current for the electric action (see Fig. 115, p. 156), but generators and electric motors hardly belong to the scope of our present survey, and we will proceed straight to the 'bellows' or, to give it its truer name, the reservoir.

The purpose of the reservoir is twofold. It stores the wind ready for use, by the pipes or action-chests, and also, by an ingenious valve and spring arrangement which we will see in a moment, it ensures that the wind-supply is maintained at a constant and specified pressure. The reservoir we are about to examine is of the most modern type (Fig. 117, p. 159). It consists of a well and a bellows section. The well is made in much the same way as the wind-chest which we have already seen. All joints and corners are carefully lined, or 'patched', to use the trade term, strips of sheepskin being glued along all joints on the inside of the 'box'.

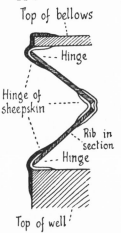

Fig. 118. *Method of hingeing ribs.*

The upper part of the reservoir is made movable by the provision of ribs hinged and covered with sheepskin. The making of the bellows involves craftsmanship of a high order, and we will therefore watch for a while a bellows-maker at work. The 'ribs' (see Fig. 118), which are sent to him from the fine mill, are carefully prepared strips of specially selected wood, usually pine, and the maker begins work by taking a pair—there are four pairs in all, corresponding with the four sides of the well.

He places the two ribs, which form a pair, side by side, and with the appropriate edges adjacent. He cuts a long narrow strip of white sheepskin and glues it lengthwise to cover the 'crack' and to overlap a sufficient distance over both ribs, thus forming a long narrow hinge: this is known as the 'first leather'. He now folds the ribs inwards so that the hinge is on the inside and glues a 'second leather' or strip along the outside joint, precisely as he did before. The two ribs are now

163

joined by a double hinge of leather, one on either side of the wood. Since the length of a strip is limited by the size of the skin, he often has to use more than one strip to cover a joint, but he overlaps them so cleverly that it is hard to detect where one length ends and the next begins.

When all the ribs are hinged the next process is to fix them to the sides of the well and also to the top of the bellows; and this is done in the same way as that just described. The next operation is, perhaps, the most difficult of all, namely, that of gusseting and strengthening the corners (Fig. 119). The bellows is propped up to its maximum rise, the angle between the

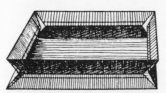

FIG. 119. *Relative position of the four sets of ribs, and corner spaces which will be covered by the gussets.*

ribs being ninety degrees ($\angle 90°$) while this is being done. Four gussets, cut ready to shape, are glued across the corner junctions of the ribs. Over each gusset is placed a strengthening layer, known as a corner-piece. This serves a double purpose: it acts as a protection against wear and gives additional strength where the maximum movement—and strain—takes place. The top of the bellows is provided with a detachable panel giving access to the valve and springs (Fig. 117, p. 159).

The wind-pressure within the reservoir is kept constant by springs whose resistance will depend upon the pressure required. External springs (Fig. 115, p. 156) may be provided, or internal springs such as those shown (Fig. 121, p. 166) may be fitted. As the bellows section of the reservoir expands, its upward movement is 'met' by the resistance of the springs, which endeavour to restrain it. But when this expansion exceeds a stipulated amount, according to the capacity and pressure required, the rising bellows operates a valve which arrests the inflowing wind. Various valves are used for this purpose, but that in common use at the moment is known as a roller valve and is an ingenious device. It consists of a box or chamber one side of which contains a grid (q.v.),

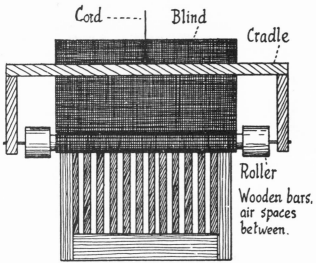

Fig. 120. *Detail of roller valve.*

i.e. a series of narrow parallel strips of wood with spaces or slots between them (Fig. 120). At one side of this grid, namely, that by which the wind from the pressure generator enters, a roller blind is suspended. The roller is raised or lowered by a cord attached to it. When the roller is 'up' the wind proceeds through the interstices of the grid, but when it is down the blind covers the apertures and the wind, pressing the blind against the bars, prevents any further air from entering.

The wind must enter the reservoir by way of this valve, which may be placed either inside or outside the well. The valve is regulated from the bellows section. A cord, attached to the 'roof' of the bellows, passes through two pulleys in such a way that when it rises the roller descends and when the expansion reaches a prescribed limit the blind completely covers the grid and so prevents any more air from entering. As the wind is used up, the bellows contract, the 'curtain' is raised, and the wind once more proceeds into the reservoir.

From the reservoir a wind-trunk of zinc tubing or of wood —of rectangular section—conducts the wind to its destination, either to the various wind-chests and so to the pipes, or to the action-chests for the manipulation of valves and motors in the pneumatic sections.

FIG. 121. *An internal spring (see* Fig. 117).

We have now traced our survey from console, via switch-stack, to action and pipes, and have followed the wind from generator to the same destination. It is quite impossible to see every kind of pipe being made, but since they are constructed either from wood or metal we will at least pay a visit to the wood-pipe and the metal-pipe departments.

Pipe-making is, of course, an art in itself and one that dates back thousands of years. We saw how wood-wind and brass instruments were made, but in each case they were designed and built to produce a whole gamut of notes within the range of the instrument. Here a pipe produces only one note, and this, though not necessarily the fundamental, is the most beautiful in tone which the designer can achieve. One of the problems will be to 'match' the tone in a series of pipes so that they form a perfect rank, homogeneous in quality and power throughout. It is not difficult to appreciate that a set of pipes may achieve, on the one hand, the highest perfection in beauty and matching of tone, while on the other the result might well, and sometimes does, approach cacophony.

An organ manual contains but five complete octaves, as

compared with the seven and a quarter octaves of the modern pianoforte keyboard. The range of the two instruments cannot be compared, however, with the number of keys, for in the case of the organ the keys, through manipulation of stops, can play ranks of pipes of widely ranging compass. Thus, the range even of smaller organs is actually eight octaves, and the maximum range is eleven octaves. The pipes themselves vary in length from thirty-two feet to three-quarters of an inch. Sixty-eight feet pipes are to be found, and so, too, are tiny pipes only three-eighths of an inch in length, but these are rare. There is, however, a sixty-four foot stop in the Sydney Town Hall organ, Australia, and there may be others in America. The lengths of pipes always refer, by the way, to the 'speaking' part of the pipe.

Organ pipes, of which there are literally thousands of different kinds, may be divided into three main groups, namely, flue pipes, reeds, and diaphones; flue pipes may further be subdivided into diapasons, flutes, and strings. Similarly, reeds may be of the solo or chorus type. Flue pipes greatly predominate in the average organ and they may be described as modified whistles: they are made of wood or of metal (Figs. 122-7, pp. 168-70). Reed pipes are usually made of metal and the sound is produced by a vibrating reed or thin metal tongue, which is placed in front of the aperture in the shallot (see Fig. 128, p. 171). Generally speaking, all wooden flue pipes are of square or rectangular section, while the metal pipes of this family are round. The reed pipes, however, which are usually made of metal, vary greatly in length and in shape. In some, the resonators are much longer than corresponding flue pipes of the same pitch, while in others, such as the *vox humana* pipes, the resonators are only about one-eighth of the normal length.

The diaphone pipes might be described as a cross between flue and reed. They have, in place of the reed, a metal vibrator (Fig. 129, p. 171). This sets up much stronger vibrations than a

167

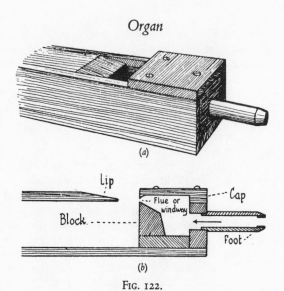

FIG. 122.

a, *Open wooden pipe*; b, *Sectional view showing construction and passage of wind.*

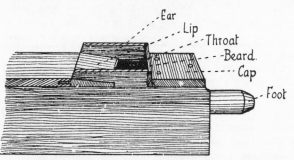

FIG. 123. *Mouth end of wood pipe such as is used for bass of pedal organ.*

reed, but diaphones can be so constructed as to produce tone qualities which closely resemble either reed or flue pipes.

Wood pipes range in size from thirty-two feet to five-eighths

of an inch in length. The largest wooden pipe in Great Britain
—i.e. that in the organ at Liverpool Cathedral—measures thirty-six feet (over all) by two feet nine
inches in width and three feet two
inches in depth: it weighs twenty-two
hundredweights. The bigger pipes
are made of Oregon pine, Douglas

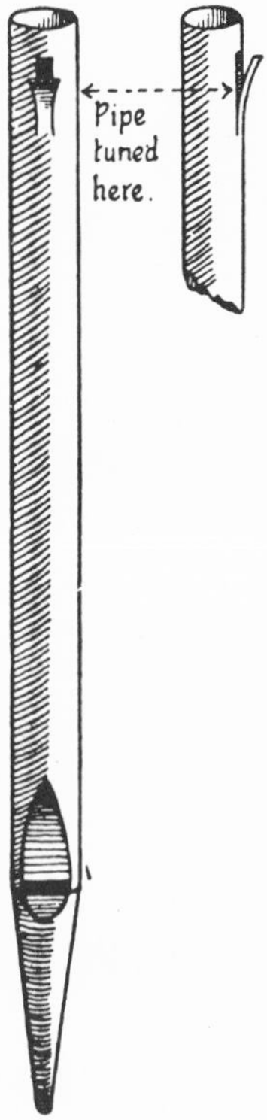

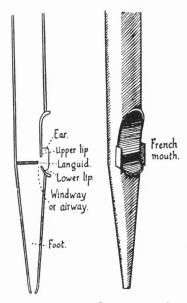

FIG. 124. *Large-scale open
diapason, which forms the
true foundation of organ tone.*

FIG. 125. *Large flue-pipe—metal—as
used for diapason stops.*

fir, or any large growing timber of good quality. The parts
come in from the mill already prepared—according to the
pipe-maker's measurements—as a complete set, each pipe being

represented by four sides tied together, so that for a complete 'stop' there will be sixty-one bundles of four—graded in length, width, and thickness according to the scale or pitch. The pipe-maker shows us his scale-board, on which are the measurements for the final finished work. It is a complicated kind of rule. He shows us also a length-rod for a stop correspond-

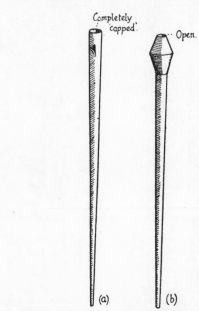

FIG. 126. *Trumpet type (cf. Trombone, Fig. 128).*

FIG. 127. *Types of resonators.*
a, *Orchestral oboe, fully capped—i.e. closed—at top;* b, *Cor anglais.*

ing to the scale-board we have just seen. He now begins to 'finish up' the various 'sides' to the measurements on the scale-board. He is most particular that the inside faces of the pipe are

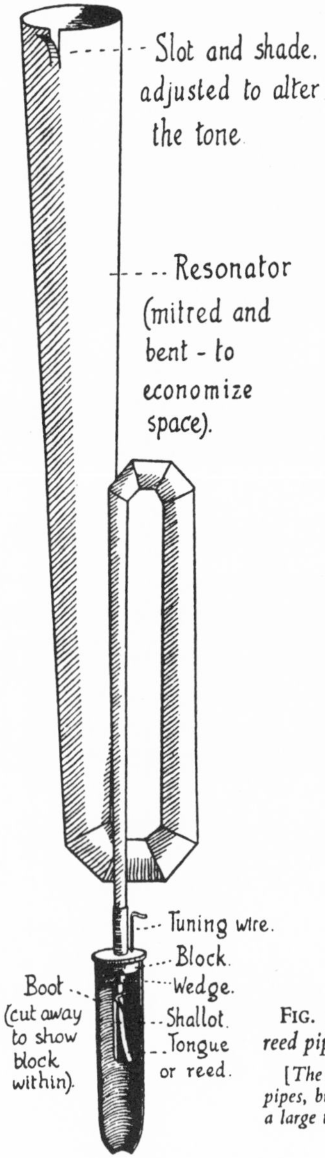

- - - Slot and shade.
adjusted to alter
the tone.

- - - Resonator
(mitred and
bent - to
economize
space).

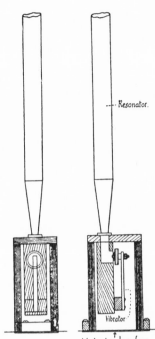

- - - Resonator.

Vibrator

Wind enters here from
sound-board when key
is depressed.

FIG. 129. *Two sectional views of a diaphone.*

- - - Tuning wire.
- - - Block.
- - - Wedge.
- - - Shallot.
- - - Tongue
or reed.

Boot - - -
(cut away
to show
block
within).

FIG. 128. *Sectional sketch showing typical reed pipe.*

[*The block and boot are much the same for all reed pipes, but the resonators vary considerably. This is a large trombone pipe.*]

accurate; to quote his own words, 'Take care of the inside and the outside will take care of itself.' He prepares two sides, and in the case of the larger pipes cuts the grooves for the blocks (see Fig. 122 b, p. 168). In making the smaller pipes the blocks are simply glued, and in some cases they are also nailed. The sides of the pipe, when completed, are fixed to the block at the foot end of the pipe and to a temporary block at the opposite end. The back and front are now fixed to the sides. Glue is used in all cases, but in the smaller pipes these are wrapped round with stout string while the glue is setting, whereas the larger pipes are either nailed or screwed in addition. The pipes are either open or 'stopped'; in the latter case they sound roughly an octave lower than when open. The stopper consists of a wooden block, which is covered with leather and is provided with a handle so that it can be adjusted for tuning purposes within the upper end of the pipe.

When the pipe is assembled it is planed up by machine if small, or by hand if large. Some pipes are provided with 'ears' and 'beards' (see Fig. 123, p. 168), and these are fitted during the assembly of the pipe. The insides of the pipes are sometimes painted or otherwise 'treated', and if they are intended for export to hot countries are painted with a special preparation to protect them against insect pests. The outsides are either painted or polished. The pipes in the swell-box are nearly always polished. Some of the pipes we see about us are of huge size, while the foreman shows us, by way of contrast, tiny pipes, perfect in every detail, which we could carry away comfortably in our coat pockets.

At this point we are asked to inspect for a moment a complete organ which is ready for dispatch. It is all pneumatic, though driven by an electric wind generator. Our guide shows us the console, complete with draw-knobs and thumb-pistons, pedals and toe-pistons. He shows us how the wind is 'stored' in three separate reservoirs, each at a different pressure. He draws our attention particularly to the third reservoir, which, though considerably smaller than either of the others, contains wind at a much higher pressure, for it is responsible for the smooth running of the pneumatic action. And now we realize for the first time that *volume* and *pressure* are by no means synonymous, for here we have in one case large capacity at comparatively low pressure, and in the other, a smaller capacity at high pressure. This is quite a small organ, but the workmanship is excellent and the whole job is a model of compact arrangement.

The great organs of to-day contain hundreds of metal pipes, which range in 'speaking-length' from thirty-two feet to three-eighths of an inch, and in diameter from two feet to three-sixteenths of an inch. The diapasons, strings, dulcianas, flutes, reeds, trumpets, trombones, tubas and clarions, clarinets and oboes are all made of metal. We go now to the metal-pipe department, where innumerable pipes, of diverse size and shape and in varied stages of disjointedness, await us. The larger pipes are made of hard-rolled sheet zinc, which is supplied to the firm either in rolls, packed in barrels, or in flat sheets contained in large wooden crates.

The smaller pipes, and those requiring particular tone quality, are made from 'metal' prepared on the premises. The pipe-makers use the word *metal* where we would mean *alloy*, i.e. a mixture of metals. In one corner of this department we see a number of ingots, each weighing about fifty-six pounds. They are of pure Cornish tin. In another are stacked lead 'pigs' of virgin lead, each weighing about a hundredweight. And here are some smaller ingots of 'type', a metal which is used as a hardening agent in the alloy, which the pipe-makers prepare for their own use.

For certain pipes, we are told, particular alloys are compounded. Spotted metal, for instance, is employed to produce particular tone effects, and when we are shown several sheets of spotted metal we notice that in some examples the spots are quite small, while in others they are larger and 'more bumpy'. This, we learn, is due to the proportion of tin to lead in the alloy; the larger the percentage of tin, the larger and more pronounced will be the spot, which is caused by the lighter metal, i.e. tin, rising to the surface prior to cooling.

We are indeed fortunate to-day, for sheet-metal is actually about to be cast. At one end of the 'casting-shop' is a small furnace where the metal is being melted. Lead, tin, and 'type' have been put into the furnace, under which a hot fire is burning, and the molten metal is 'just about ready'.

A long table, or bench, extends almost from one end of the casting-shop to the other. It is a curious table, for it consists of a *single solid* slab of stone, fourteen or fifteen feet long, a yard wide, and six inches thick, supported on legs of great strength. Such a stone, hewn in one piece, must have cost a great deal of money. We do not *see* the stone until we ask to do so, for it is covered with fustian cloth, and over that is a further covering of fine quality-linen. This is used to protect the stone slab from being burned. Stone is used because it does not warp under the hot metal.

At the end of the bench nearest the furnace is a hinged ladle (see Fig. 130, p. 175), which rests in a special frame attached to the bench. On the table itself is placed a gauge (Fig. 131, p. 176). It is made of Spanish mahogany and consists of a box without top or bottom. It fits exactly the width of the bench and has a guard, or guide, at one side to keep it true to the edge of the bench. The end simply holds the frame of the 'box' together, but inside this there is an adjustable board which can be raised or lowered by means of screw adjusters, so that sheets of metal ranging in thickness from half an inch to that of lead foil may be cast, according to the adjustment of the board. The inside of the gauge is treated with black-lead to prevent the wood being burned by the molten metal.

At the end of the bench nearest the furnace is a raised bar against which the gauge rests. There is also a length of fustian which protects the stone from the intense heat of the molten metal. At the far end of the table is a well into which the surplus metal will fall as soon as the gauge reaches it.

Now all is ready for the 'cast'. The foreman takes up a long

Tilting ladle

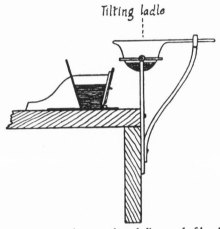

FIG. 130. *Sectional view showing tilting ladle at end of bench, and gauge, in position it occupies while being filled.*

ladle and proceeds to fill the hinged ladle or pouring-pot with molten metal from the furnace. He then takes a small ladle and begins to stir the silvery liquid. If this is too hot he cools it slightly by melting strips of cold metal in the tilting ladle. Constantly he stirs, watching the metal very closely, and occasionally ladling off the scum which keeps rising to the surface of the liquid. Now he is 'on the look-out' for 'stars' or 'grit', which will soon be rising to the surface. The appearance of these specks tells him that the metal is reaching the critical temperature, and that the crucial moment for casting is at hand. Suddenly he makes a sign to his assistant, who takes his place at the gauge. The foreman tilts the ladle so that all the

175

metal contained therein is poured into the gauge. Immediately the two men, one at each side of the table, walk rapidly along with the gauge between them. As they go we see behind the gauge a sheet of shining white metal lying on the table. The

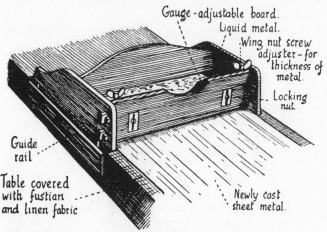

Gauge-adjustable board.

Liquid metal.

Wing nut screw adjuster - for thickness of metal.

Locking nut.

Guide rail

Table covered with fustian and linen fabric

Newly cast sheet metal.

FIG. 131. *Gauge, leaving behind it the sheet of metal.*

whole process takes only about four seconds. When the gauge reaches the far end the men slightly raise it as they approach the well, and the surplus metal is deposited there. The most curious thing about the whole process is that no metal has overflowed at the sides of the table, for there is no ridge nor raised edge of any kind to confine the metal. The explanation is, perhaps, that the metal at the extreme edge cools so quickly that it 'sets' before it has time to flow over the sides, and also that the foreman is able to judge the temperature so accurately as to ensure a successful cast.

Meanwhile the newly cast metal has cooled, and dulled. Its sheen has faded, and a silver-grey sheet of metal remains. Soon it is cool enough to handle, and the foreman cuts off the two thick' ends, as he calls them, for the ends are irregular. He uses a special cutting tool and a straight edge, cutting partially through the metal and then breaking off the unwanted piece. The men now roll it up like a carpet and, after weighing it, stand it upright among numerous rolls already placed there. This process is repeated again and again. The 'cast-up' may last for two or three whole days, and may occur at intervals of three weeks or a month.

One thing we notice here is that the atmosphere is very close. We ask why the windows are all closed and are told that to open them would allow cold air to enter, which would ruin the job. What makes it worse is that tallow is melted along with the metal, in order to help to purify the metal by facilitating the rise of scum to the surface.

The foreman tells us that he works out the thickness of each sheet by the weight of metal he uses, and so he refers to a certain roll as being so many pounds (weight). Each roll is placed on the scale and its weight entered on a special list before being stacked ready for use.

We are taken now to the metal pipe-makers' department. Here at benches are makers working at pipes of all sizes and shapes and in various stages of completion. (A few of the commoner types of metal pipe are shown at Figs. 124-8.) First the maker takes a rectangular strip of metal, which he proceeds to plane down to the requisite thickness. He uses for this purpose a plane very like a joiner's jack-plane, but he shows us that the blade is sharpened in quite a different way and is set at a more acute angle, i.e. it is more vertical. After this first planing, he takes up a hand scraper, which removes a fine shaving, and continues to scrape the metal, testing the surface and thickness with his fingers. All these men work solely by touch and never use a measuring instrument of any kind for testing the thickness of the metal.

The next process is to get a cylindrical mandril, of which there is a complete set corresponding to the 'stop' he is making.

N

He rolls the metal round this mandril and beats it to shape with a hard-wood beater, made from lignum vitae, until the adjacent edges are touching. He then removes the mandril and paints a band of special 'size' along the edges, which he will later solder together, 'to keep the solder within the limits of the seam', as he terms it. When the size has dried, he uses a sharp-pointed knife to cut the two edges so that an angle is formed between them of slightly more than ninety degrees. He takes up a heavy copper soldering-bit which he has previously heated, and after applying a flux which somewhat resembles a wax candle he 'tacks' along the joint, that is to say, he puts little beads of solder at intervals all along the joint to hold it in position. He then proceeds to solder the joint from end to end between the tacks. When the solder has cooled he cleans off the size and the joint is completed. The part he has just made is the resonator or cylindrical portion of the pipe.

We ask him next to show us how he does the conical section, or foot, and how he makes the mouth. First he marks out the shape on a sheet of metal, using a ruler and scribe; the 'pattern' looks like a segment of a circle. He turns this round the appropriate conical wooden mandril, beats it to shape, solders it just as he did the other joint, but before doing so flattens one part of the cone on a lipping tool, which consists of a wooden mandril partially flattened and having a metal face screwed to it. When the conical or foot section is complete the languid (Fig. 125, p. 169) is cut to fit the wide end and soldered to it. The foot section is now soldered to the resonator and the pipe is complete.

Large pipes are made of zinc, and these are rolled by a special machine consisting of two large rollers with a third behind them, which can be so adjusted that the curve of the sheet to be rolled can be controlled in such a way that it will be of the diameter required.

Before leaving the pipe-makers there is just one more job we would like to see. Here is a craftsman making tiny pipes, some of which are only about half the thickness of an ordinary lead pencil—the actual 'speaking' portions are less than an inch long. He is preparing a sheet of very thin metal shaped something like a pennant flag, i.e. tapering from one end to the other. He is 'thinning down' the sheet so that as it tapers from the wide to the narrow end it becomes also gradually thinner and thinner. All the processes he uses are the same as those we have seen, but in spite of the Lilliputian scale to which he is working we see, when he hands us a completed pipe, quite the tiniest we have ever seen, that each detail is exquisitely finished. The miniature langui dand mouth, the finely soldered joints, are all perfectly executed. There are many varieties of metal pipes which we would like to see made, such as those shown (pp. 170, 171), but we must move on once more, this time to the voicing department. We have seen many pipes being made, but have not heard one sounding. They do not 'speak' until they have been through the hands of the voicer. In the voicing room is a rather curious instrument known as the voicing machine. It is really a complete organ with keyboard, wind-chest, and upper board; in the latter are numerous pipe-holes into which the voicer places the pipes. The whole instrument is arranged so as to facilitate access to keyboard and pipes. At one end of the manual is an extension consisting of a miniature keyboard from which the sixteen-foot pipes of the Pedal organ are played. These pipes are voiced on a separate sound-board placed low down and to one side of the voicing machine, which itself cannot accommodate pipes of more than eight feet. The thirty-two-foot pipes are voiced in the large assembly room, and where possible on their own sound-board.

The voicer's first concern is the particular pitch required for the organ to which the pipes belong and the exact pressure of the wind. He first adjusts the pressure of his 'machine' to the required degree and then places a pitch-pipe in a special wind hole. This pipe gives him the actual pitch—usually 'the one-foot C', as he terms it (we would call it 'Middle C'). From this note he tunes another set of pipes, in this case a complete octave in the key of G, from the G above to that below middle C. This becomes his standard for all the pipes belonging to the particular organ being built. Some tuners prepare a complete range of sixty-one notes for this purpose, but our voicer uses only the octave we have mentioned.

In organ-building, the word 'scale' has a special meaning. It refers to the area of the cross-section of a pipe in relation to its length. In the case of cylindrical pipes the scale would be expressed in terms of the length and diameter. Thus, four foot of three-inch scale would signify a pipe four feet long by three inches in diameter. With wooden pipes both width and depth are given with the length.

The voicer first tunes his 'standard octave'. This is composed of flue pipes, and each has a tuning-slot at the upper end of it, while over this is fitted a short outer casing provided with a projecting arm which the tuner can tap upwards or downwards, and thereby adjust the pitch. He now proceeds to voice and tune a complete rank of pipes, placing them in their appropriate pipe-holes while he does so and taking them out occasionally to make an adjustment. We ask him to tell us just what he *does* to the pipes, and he has some difficulty in explaining his work, not for a moment because he does not *know*, but because his art is so intangible: almost it requires a sixth sense. He explains that 'reeds' and flue pipes are totally different, and so is the method of voicing and tuning them. Let us consider a reed pipe first (Fig. 128, p. 171). The reed, or tongue, is the most important factor here. It is made of a special kind of hard-rolled brass, of a thickness or gauge suitable for the type of reed required, and supplied in rolls. The voicer is very careful when cutting the tongue to see that this is done along the curve of the roll, and not across it. The strip is curved on an appliance which resembles a rigid razor-strop, and the tool used comprises a round steel rod, of about the thickness of an ordinary pencil, with a handle at each end. He lays the reed, clamped at one end, on the 'strop' and strokes it firmly towards the other, causing the reed to curl slightly. Both the thickness of the metal and the nature of the curve are of extreme importance. When completed, the tongue is held in position on the shallot by means of a wedge of hard wood or fibre driven with the shallot and tongue into the block.

When voicing and tuning the pipe he fits on the resonator, places the foot in a pipe-hole, and by means of the tuning-wire, which he moves up and down, adjusts the tongue until he is satisfied with the resultant tone.

In the case of flue pipes (Figs. 124, 125, p. 169), the voicer begins by adjusting the height of the lower lip, or the 'cut-up', as he terms it. He then adjusts the width of the flue, or air-channel. The process which follows is known as 'nicking the languid'. He uses special tools for all these processes and they are all 'home-made', as he terms it. The nicking tool is a specially shaped and sharpened steel blade let into a handle, and with it he makes a series of tiny nicks in the front edge of the languid. Just how many of these he makes, or how deep they are, he cannot define; he works by a kind of instinct which he has acquired through long experience.

To digress for a moment, he tells us here that he has spent all his 'working life' in this factory, that his father, who recently retired and is now seventy-eight, spent sixty years with this firm, and that his grandfather was also a voicer here before him. He adds naïvely, 'Voicers are not made in a day!'

The fifth and final process is to adjust the upper lip in correct relationship, by means of a lipping tool. It must not be thought that each of these processes is independent of the others; it would be truer to say that all are interdependent, affecting one another in varying degree.

The nicking, for instance, will have the effect of causing the concentrated 'edge' of wind passing through the airway or windway (see Fig. 125, p. 169) to waver, or to be slightly disturbed in a deliberate way, and this will affect the distance at which the upper lip, upon which this issuing air-current will impinge, shall be fixed. Other similar inter-relationships will arise, but further complications we will leave for the voicer to solve.

The voicing of wood pipes is similar to that just described for metal flue pipes. The same processes are involved, but the tools used are, of course, those we associate with the working of wood. The languid is replaced by the block (see Fig. 122 b, p. 168) and the flue can be adjusted at the cap, which can be easily removed, being simply screwed into position. 'Nicking' is done with the aid of a tool with a short saw-edge at the end of it.

We may now sum up the voicer's aim, as far as each single pipe is concerned: it is to adjust the mouth of the pipe so as to ensure prompt and pure speech. But his work does not end here. He must also even up his tone so that the whole *set* of pipes will *speak* as one instrument.

The adjustment for power or dynamic is done at the foot of the pipe, and where this is of metal the aperture is made smaller, and consequently the tone softer, by the use of a 'knocking-up cup', a cone-shaped cup of gun-metal, which, when placed over the open end of the foot and hammered, reduces the size of the aperture, which can be increased, if greater power is required, by being enlarged with a reamer. Large wood pipes are regulated for intensity of tone by means of a vane or 'fan', which consists of a metal disk the size of the inside bore, which is mounted on a central pivot and can be turned at any angle within the pipe, thus controlling the amount of wind passing through it. The majority of wood pipes are provided with a block or stopping which is inserted into the foot and is so shaped as to allow the exact amount of wind desired to pass into the pipe.

Here we must take our leave of the voicer for a while, but

we shall see him again, for his work is by no means finished. His final voicing and tuning must be done *in the building which is to house the finished organ.*

In the meantime we are taken to the assembly-room, which is the largest and most spacious department in the whole factory. In size it would compare with many large concert-halls, both in height and extent. Here the organ is assembled. First the building frame for the main organ is constructed and assembled. This has been designed to accommodate the complete instrument and also to fit the space allocated in accordance with the dimensions of the building in which the organ is to be installed.

Within the frame mentioned above, the sound-boards and actions, the wind reservoirs, together with the wind-trunks connecting them, are assembled. The swell-boxes are also installed. These are chambers constructed of sound-proof material and enclosing the pipes. Their action has already been described and they are controlled from the swell pedals. In modern organs the opening and closing of the louvres or shutters is balanced by the use of weights, springs, or other means, so that the pedal can be depressed to any desired degree and left in that position. At one time the organist had to hold down the pedal or fix it under a 'swinging stick' provided with a notch and known as the swell 'catch'. But even so, when manipulating this, or while holding down the pedal, he had only one foot available for controlling his pedal key-board and accessories.

The smaller pipes are next assembled and the various adjustments are completed. The larger pipes are not put in as a rule until the instrument is finally set up in the building in which it is destined to remain.

In the case of the smaller pneumatic organs, where the console is 'built in', all the tubular wind-connexions are completed. With the larger electro-pneumatic and pneumatic organs, however, the console is detached, and in this case is completed as a separate unit, but the connexions, whether they be tubes or wires, are not completed.

The final stage has now been reached. The instrument is carefully taken down and packed into special containers for transport by road, rail, or sea to its destination. Here it is unpacked and re-assembled, as before, but now all fixtures and connexions are made permanent. We need not dwell upon the final stages of finishing and overhauling to be carried out, but we must have another talk with the voicer-finisher, who, with his assistant, is the last man to work on the instrument. To him is left the important task of toning-up the whole organ, and where this is a large one the work may occupy him for a whole month.

All churches and halls have their own peculiar acoustic properties, and no one can predict just how the newly assembled organ will react to them. We have met the subject of resonation already, and since a hall or church is, to a certain extent, an enclosed space, it is apt to act as a resonator. But this propensity, which is practically beyond control, may well be an unfortunate one. The voicer, for instance, may find that all his C's, especially those at a certain pitch, are 'booming' because of the fact that there is a sympathetic vibration in the building which responds to and amplifies all notes in the vicinity of this particular pitch. The voicer will have to tone down all the pipes which are so affected in one of the ways he showed us in the voicing department.

Another problem may confront him: one particular stop may predominate in such a way as to upset the balance of the whole instrument. The cause may be due to some acoustic vagary, or to a freak of sound-reflection causing an echo, or it may be just inexplicable. Whatever the cause, the voicer must go over the complete range of pipes concerned, and tone them down. It might happen, again, that a stop which seemed loud enough in the voicing-room sounds feeble here, so that he must increase the power of the pipes concerned.

Organ

Thus the voicer, starting with the Principal stop, tests each note with the greatest care and gradually matches or builds up the other stops, first one by one and then in combination, listening and testing all the time for 'balance and matching of power and tone', to quote his own words. And here we will leave him to complete his work.

At last we stand before the finished organ, but the story is not complete, for the organ-stool is vacant. Anon comes the organist, who takes his place, moves here a switch and there a draw-knob. At his command the instrument comes to life, its majestic tones proclaiming that the voicer has truly completed his work. It is perhaps at this moment that we realize for the first time the true meaning of the word *organ*, which we have used so many times. Here, surely, is an 'instrument of musick' of which the fabric blends so well with its surroundings and its tone with the very atmosphere of the place as to become both in silence and in sound an integral part of the edifice to which it belongs.

Before concluding our survey of organ manufacture a word must be said and a tribute paid to those who have remained 'behind the scenes', but whose work, nevertheless, is perhaps the most important of all, namely, the real creators, the designers and draughtsmen who plan these wonderful instruments, set out the details of each and every part, work out the most intricate measurements, and draw all those plans which we have seen during our many visits to the factory. It is, indeed, due to them that these visits have been made possible. To them, to their colleagues in all the other factories where we have been, to their managers and foremen, and, last but not least, to the countless craftsmen whom we have watched at their work, we tender our grateful thanks and bid a reluctant farewell.

A NOTE ON ELECTRONICS

DURING the last few years a number of scientists and inventors have been engaged in exploring the possibilities of the science of electronics, which is concerned with the production and control, electrically, of sound. Several outstanding examples of the practical application of electronics might be mentioned, but to us the most interesting is the creation of pipeless 'organs'. In some of these instruments the sound is produced by means of oscillations generated by valves, while in others revolving disks are used to set up periodic impulses in a magnetic field.

Of the latter variety, the most advanced instrument we have yet encountered is known as the Hammond organ, which is being demonstrated and sold in this country. There is reason to believe that at least one London firm of organ-builders is constructing an instrument on similar lines which will surpass the existing American model. At the same time, it must be observed that the Hammond organ, and others of a similar kind, are in their infancy, and, to pursue the analogy, when these infants of a mere year or two really 'grow up', as they might do, very rapidly, we may possibly find them seriously challenging the traditional pipe-organ in the near future.

The electronic organ which we heard and played some time ago is the invention of Laurens Hammond, a prominent inventor, of Chicago. It is entirely electric, having no pipes of any kind and, consequently, no wind supply. It consists of a console, somewhat smaller than an upright pianoforte, and a sound-cabinet of about the same size, the two components being connected by a flexible cable.

The most important unit of the instrument is the tone-wheel (see Fig. 132, p. 187). This is a metallic disk having a number of facets or edges, and between them corners, or 'high spots'. There are ninety-one graduated disks, mounted on a common spindle, driven by the same synchronous motor. Since they are carefully graduated, they produce ninety-one different tones, or, to put it a better way, the same tone at ninety-one different pitches.

Now let us try to understand just how these disks can pro-

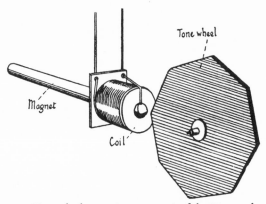

FIG. 132. *Tone-wheel—most important unit of the Hammond organ.*

duce tones. Closely adjacent to each tone-wheel is a permanent magnet, having one end wound with wire. When a disk rotates, the corners, or high spots, as they pass the magnet, induce a tiny current in the coil adjacent to it. Suppose a disk be rotating in such way that five hundred high spots are passing the magnet every second. The impulses so caused set up a minute alternating current of this frequency in the coil and its circuit. If head-phones could be connected we should hear a musical note corresponding in pitch to a frequency of five hundred vibrations per second. If the next disk were made so that at the same speed of rotation four hundred and eighty high spots per second were passing the corresponding magnet, we should hear a lower note. Once this principle is understood it becomes clear that if the disks are so graduated that any desired series of frequencies can be obtained, a corresponding range of 'notes' will be produced. These electrical impulses are 'magnified' in a pre-amplifier in the console and then proceed to vacuum tube amplifiers in the power cabinet, where the current is translated by speakers into musical sound.

At this point it is necessary to explain how the various tone qualities corresponding to the stops of the pipe-organ are obtained. It has long been known to musicians and to scientists that the tone-quality and timbre of voices, pipes, brass instruments, and so forth is due to the presence and nature of the harmonics, or upper partials, which are present when the root or fundamental note is sounding. Within the limits of this instrument, that is precisely how the tone for any particular stop is obtained: tone-quality is built up synthetically.

On the console there are two manuals, each containing sixty-one playing notes. At the extreme left there are two complete octaves of keys, whose colours are reversed, i.e. the usual white keys are replaced by black ones, and the black, by white keys. These are press-keys, which take the place of the draw-knobs on a pipe-organ. Each key represents a stop, such as dulciana, diapason, tromba, and so forth, and they are pre-set by a simple wiring device in the console. An organist can choose which stops he prefers, and these can be arranged and pre-set. Each stop-key, when pressed, automatically cuts out and replaces the existing stop in action. In addition, above the upper manual there are thirty-eight draw-bars which control the harmonics. Each one can be set at eight different positions, numbered from zero to eight and representing eight degrees of intensity for the particular harmonic concerned.

Of the stop-keys at the left of each manual, the extreme key in each case is a cancel key, while at the extreme right of the key-stops are switch-keys connecting the manuals with their harmonic controllers.

In addition to the eighteen pre-set keys, the organist can

manipulate the harmonic controls independently, building up stops to suit his own taste.

To take an example, suppose he wishes to make full trumpet tone. He has a fairly clear idea of the harmonic nature of the tone he requires, and he begins by playing a fundamental note which, by the way, is very like the flute in quality. To this he adds the upper partials (8th, 15th, &c.) by drawing out the particular draw-bars to the various strengths he requires. After a little experimenting he finds a combination which satisfies him and jots it down for future reference.

When we asked a demonstrator to 'make' an oboe, clarinet, trumpet, or trombone, he found the correct combination very quickly and the resultant tone was surprisingly faithful.

A 'mixture' stop, representing, for example, diapason with brass and reeds, can similarly be obtained. Perhaps the most pleasing feature of the instrument is the balanced swell pedal, which is probably the most sensitive and efficient yet devised. It can shade the tone from a whisper, almost, to a *crescendo* which is literally enormous.

There are naturally one or two points where improvements will no doubt be made. The addition of more tone-wheels, representing an increase in the number of upper partials available, would tend to enhance the range in tone-colour and would improve, perhaps, the diapason tone, which does not quite reach the standard attained by a pipe-organ. In addition, coupling might be incorporated so that existing pre-set stops could be used in combination. As it is, only one stop can be played on each manual, or on the pedals, at a time.

But, as we have said, the instrument 'has only just been born' and its possibilities seem to be almost without limit. Whether it will ever seriously challenge 'our old friend' the pipe-organ is a question we will leave unanswered.

Since going to press we have received information of an improved model of the Hammond organ which has several notable improvements on the model already described: particularly, a thirty-two note concave and radiating pedal clavier, separate adjustable 'tremulants' and expression—or swell—pedals for each manual, and a Great-to-Pedal coupler. There is also a new type of console whereon the reverse coloured black and white press-keys already discussed have been superseded by pistons, each with its own 'stop' name.

In addition, there is a *Chorus Generator*. We cannot describe this in detail, but one feature is of interest. To quote from the text of the brochure: 'The chorus generator has its own starting and running motors which operate simultaneously with the motors of the main generator.

'To each of certain tone-wheels in the main generator there is, in the chorus generator, a pair of tone-wheels which have their speeds so adjusted that one will produce a tone slightly sharp, and the other a tone slightly flat, by comparison with the accurately tuned main generator frequencies.

'Thus, when the chorus generator is turned on, and a single frequency sounded from the main generator, the two slightly de-tuned chorus frequencies will also sound, and the result is the formation of a complex series of "beats" or "waves" in the tone.'

This quotation is interesting in the light of what we learned in the tuners' room (p. 112).

Moreover, it gives some idea of the potentiality of the pipeless organ.